MISS
LEARNING

D0200915

DATE DUE

Partners in Education

Theodore L. Gross

Partners in Education

*How Colleges Can Work
with Schools to Improve
Teaching and Learning*

Jossey-Bass Publishers
San Francisco   •   London   •   1988

PARTNERS IN EDUCATION
How Colleges Can Work with Schools to Improve Teaching and Learning
  by Theodore L. Gross

Copyright © 1988 by: Jossey-Bass Inc., Publishers
                    350 Sansome Street
                    San Francisco, California 94104
                          &
                    Jossey-Bass Limited
                    28 Banner Street
                    London EC1Y 8QE

Copyright under International, Pan American, and
Universal Copyright Conventions. All rights
reserved. No part of this book may be reproduced
in any form—except for brief quotation (not to
exceed 1,000 words) in a review or professional
work—without permission in writing from the publishers.

The list of twenty-two fundamental economic concepts that
appears on pages 115–116 is taken from *A Framework for Teaching
the Basic Concepts,* copyright © 1977, 1984, by the Joint
Council on Economic Education. Reprinted by permission.

Library of Congress Cataloging-in-Publication Data

Gross, Theodore L.
    Partners in education.

    (A Joint publication in the Jossey-Bass higher
education series and the Jossey-Bass education series)
    Bibliography: p.
    Includes index.
    1. College-school cooperation—United States.
2. Education—United States—Aims and objectives.
I. Title.   II. Series: Jossey-Bass higher education
series.   III. Series: Jossey-Bass education series.
LB2331.53.G76   1988   378'.103   87-46344
ISBN 1-55542-089-3

Manufactured in the United States of America

The paper in this book meets the guidelines for
permanence and durability of the Committee on
Production Guidelines for Book Longevity of the
Council on Library Resources.

JACKET DESIGN BY WILLI BAUM

FIRST EDITION

Code 8816

LB
2331.53
.G76

A joint publication in
The Jossey-Bass
Higher Education Series
and
The Jossey-Bass
Education Series

Consulting Editor
Teaching and Learning

Kenneth E. Eble
University of Utah

Contents

Preface

Since the appearance of *A Nation at Risk* (The National Commission on Excellence in Education, 1983), the rhetoric of protest against American schools and colleges has rarely been more insistent. Dozens of reports by educational leaders such as Adler (1982), Boyer (1983), Goodlad (1984), and Sizer (1984) have documented declining achievement; they and others have recommended measures that are reflected in statewide programs that endeavor to stem the tide of mediocrity. The clamor for school reform and higher academic standards has led to benefits for teachers and some modest improvement in student achievement, but the American school system cannot accomplish the required educational reform on its own. Only by involving other constituents of our society—colleges, corporations, communities, and governmental agencies—will we be successful. Of all of these, colleges and universities are in the best position to initiate and carry out educational programs. *Partners in Education* contains a blueprint for action, which calls on institutions of higher learning to assume a leadership role in forming collaborations that will create for the field of education what Gwendolyn Brooks once invoked for the society as a whole—a mutual estate.

Until the 1980s we lived in a divided state. Business leaders paid taxes and expected educators to supply them with well-prepared graduates. Government felt little obligation to encourage state or national agendas that promoted educational partnerships. Parents did not participate professionally in the schools, and school board members were largely uninformed about the academic concerns of the school systems whose budgets they determined. Far fewer students went on to college, and schools of education—at both undergraduate and graduate levels—were as separate from colleges of liberal arts and sciences as many professional schools. In this divided state, education was not considered central to the future of the nation. In the current collaboration of social, cultural, and economic institutions, there is a somber acknowledgment—especially by business and government leaders—that only through improving the quality of learning in the United States will our nation no longer be at risk. We know now that our future is mutual and that it is being nurtured at our schools, colleges, and universities.

Within the educational field itself, there have also been fragmentation and dissatisfaction. For years, college faculties have complained about the inadequate preparation of students. But the training of teachers and the encouragement of interaction between college-level and high school educators have been considered almost exclusively the responsibility of schools of education, which are too often viewed with detachment, if not disdain, by colleges of liberal arts and sciences. The colleges themselves have been castles on a hill, walled off from the high schools and preparatory schools that send them students, the businesses that hire their graduates, and the communities in which their students live.

Ernest Boyer describes the situation succinctly: "Today, with all the talk about educational excellence, schools and colleges still live in two separate worlds. Presidents and deans rarely talk to principals and district superintendents. College faculty do not meet with their counterparts in public schools, and curriculum reforms at every level are planned in isolation. It's such a simple point—the need for close collaboration—and yet it is a priority that has been consistently ignored. Universities pretend they can have quality without working with the schools, which are, in fact, the foundation of everything universities do" (Boyer, 1985, p. 11).

Institutions of higher learning can no longer afford to remain aloof; except for highly selective colleges and universities, they need greater enrollments in order to survive, and they require corporate aid for what is often called a *margin of excellence*. Recruitment and retention of students are major preoccupations in higher education, and competition for a share of the diminishing population of college-age students has prompted administrators and faculty members to talk to their colleagues in the schools. The dialogue is often awkward, for the two cultures are systemically different and have been historically distant toward one another. But whatever the motivation and however difficult collaboration may be, there is a recognized need for sharing concerns—for partnerships.

These alliances must now include corporations, all levels of government, and communities. And though relationships may seem tenuous at first, they are essential. A college or university is the ideal constituent to create academic relationships with secondary schools, to sort out educational priorities with corporate classrooms, and to engage citizens in partnership projects that affect their communities. Colleges and universities—unlike high schools, corporations, and community agencies—are structured to develop educational partnerships. They have academic departments and faculty who educate future teachers and who carry on their own research; they house offices of external affairs and development, through which fund raising can occur; and they organize alumni and citizen groups eager to participate in educational partnerships. Colleges must now view the development and administration of educational partnerships as a central aspect of their mission, as an obligation to the society they serve, and as an opportunity to establish an agenda for action that no school system, corporation, community agency, or government can realize alone.

Audience

The primary audience for *Partners in Education* includes college presidents, vice-presidents, deans, continuing education directors, and higher education officers who serve as liaisons between their institutions and the business and governmental communities. I am particularly interested in addressing chief academic officers of colleges and universities, for educational partnerships should be under their direct leadership. They set the academic values and control the reward systems of their institutions and can initiate college/school collaborations most effectively. Obviously, I hope this book will be of interest to secondary school superintendents and teachers as well. It is important to note at the outset that my point of view is that of a college dean. My entire career has been in higher education, as an English department faculty member and an administrator in a college of liberal arts and sciences. My professional knowledge and appreciation of the American school culture has been gained primarily through leadership of the SUNY (State University of New York) Purchase Westchester School Partnership. My own awakening to the opportunities and responsibilities of educational partnerships and my ever-increasing respect for the teachers and administrators with whom I have interacted will prove, I trust, of interest to colleagues in academic administration who feel a deep concern about the state of the American educational system.

Overview of the Contents

Chapter One focuses on the possible development of partnerships in American education. It presents an overview of those that have been initiated, their scope and purposes, and their current status. It is not my intention to write a history of college/school collaborations, but by describing the most successful of them I hope to define the historical and geographical contexts in which these collaborations can be effective. The partnerships I describe include the National Writing Project, organized by the School of Education at the University of California, Berkeley; Syracuse University's Project Advance; the Yale–New Haven Teachers Institute; the Boston Compact; the National Faculty; the Academic Alliance Movement; and the National Network for Educational Renewal at the University of Washington, which involves twelve geographically diverse universities and their nearby public school districts. By examining the variety of partnerships that have been initiated and are currently thriving in this country, we begin to realize that a major force is transforming the very nature of American education. These partnerships represent a kind of cultural maturity, which acknowledges the need for collaboration in an age when schools and colleges continue to compete for increasingly scarce resources, especially teachers.

In Chapters Two and Three, I explain how educational partnerships can be organized and what administrative features determine their success. In addition to the critical role played by a college dean or chief academic officer, these features include the active leadership of secondary school superintendents; the conscious development of harmonious relations with state-funded organizations and neighboring colleges; the creation of mutual respect among teachers at all levels of education; and the responsibilities fulfilled by the executive director, project directors, proposal writers, donors, evaluators, community members and parents, advisory committees, retired executives, and government. By clarifying the distinctive roles of the five major partners of any meaningful educational collaboration—the college or university, schools, corporations, community, and governmental agencies—I recommend the methods that lead to successful partnerships.

Chapter Four is devoted to the financial aspects of partnerships: funding, fund raising, management, the special role of donors, and institutionalization of the collaboration. Every partnership must be engaged in the development of funding proposals to corporations, foundations, and public agencies, and every primary donor wants to watch his or her seed money flower into a venture that is of benefit to others. Most colleges and universities share common concerns: the budget is always tight; there are never sufficient funds for supplies and equipment; the best-laid plans are inevitably controlled by limited resources. The growth of educational partnerships depends on external funding, and the results of fund raising have a liberating effect on faculty and administrators. Grant proposals are strengthened by their association with school districts, and fund raising for

partnerships benefits the associated college or university by providing funds for the purchase of supplies and equipment, which
can be shared by the faculty.

I am also concerned in Chapter Four with one of the more
difficult dimensions of any partnership—its institutionalization
at a college or university and at secondary schools. Too often
everyone concerned with educational partnerships indulges in
scapegoating—colleges and universities blame schools, which
blame legislators, who blame the educational establishment in
general, while bewildered communities watch with wary eyes.
Furthermore, the rhetoric adds a sense of urgency: we are a
nation at risk; we need a Marshall Plan for education; illiteracy
is crippling our democracy; science education is in dangerous
decline; the at-risk student is beyond recall. However justified
this rhetoric may be, it has limited practical value. We need
solutions that work by building on or suggesting sensitive, intelligent modifications of the current structures in our society,
including our educational system.

Chapters Five through Nine deal with a variety of approaches to initiating partnerships. Each approach is presented
at some length. In describing these various agendas for action,
I often use the SUNY Purchase Westchester School Partnership,
which I have helped to administer, as a point of reference and
as one specific application. But these chapters are saved from
parochialism because this partnership's programs are similar
to those of other collaborations. In designing the SUNY Purchase Westchester School Partnership, we adapted the most
successful models to our own needs, and I would hope that
organizers of other partnerships will do the same. Moreover,
the programs we selected as models are central to American
education generally. In these five chapters, I address the motivation of students and teachers; the development of programs for
gifted as well as at-risk pupils; the improvement of teaching in
science, initially, and then in the social sciences, humanities,
and esthetics; the connection between the worlds of work and
school, enacted through a program for guidance counselors; and,
finally, the development of leadership training for superintendents, principals, teachers, school board members, college ad-

ministrators and faculty, students, managers and executives in local businesses, and leaders of social, governmental, and community agencies.

Chapter Ten is a summary of the specific recommendations I have made in this volume. I argue that a future that features partnerships as one of the most significant developments in contemporary education will offer a rare opportunity for creating cultural coherence. One of our major national problems is a lack of cultural integration—within our families and our institutions—and education can suggest a way to bring it about. Educational partnerships, in their very structure and raison d'être, are integrated—and can be successful only if they foster coherence. By forming partnerships that involve leaders from colleges, schools, corporations, governmental agencies, and communities, we can at least partially resolve or attenuate some of our most serious educational problems without threatening the autonomy of any of these participants.

Partnerships will always be confederations of constituents, precisely because each participant has a primary allegiance. Partnerships can never be coerced; their greatest virtue stems from service to society rather than self, from mutual interaction and support, and from perceiving the larger configuration instead of just one isolated part. College administrators and faculty members must take a leadership role in shaping this new configuration. As *Partners in Education* demonstrates, the effect of college/school collaborations—strengthened by association with corporations, communities, and government—can be very powerful indeed and lead toward a reformation of American education.

Purchase, New York   Theodore L. Gross
February 1988

Acknowledgments

As someone entirely acculturated to higher education, I have found my four years of association with the SUNY (State University of New York) Purchase Westchester School Partnership a transformative learning experience. I am particularly indebted to the partnership's "founding superintendents": Donald Batista, Joseph Carbone, Barry Farnham, Robert Hemberger, Richard Lerer, Thomas Maguire, Jerry Marcus, Harry Mix, William Prattella, and Ronald D. Valenti. Others have since led specific partnership programs: Henry Bangser, Murray Blueglass, and James Gaddy.

Scores of teachers and faculty members have collaborated with school superintendents, the executive director of the partnership, and me in a network of collegiality, and some emerged as leaders of projects: Felicity Dell 'Aquila and Mary Beth Anderson, who shaped the arts bridging the curriculum program; Peter Bell, who directed the Economics Center; Maria Gagliardo, who organized the Foreign Languages Institute; Barbara Mason, who returned from retirement to lead the guidance, at-risk, and retired executive programs; Marjorie Miller, who guided the Young Purchase Scholars program; and John Jay Russell and Charles Colletti, who directed the Institute for Motivation. Of all my faculty colleagues, I am most indebted to Carlo Parravano, a model clinical professor, who developed the Center for Science and Mathematics Education with his associate, Marjorie Erf.

I was most fortunate to have colleagues from foundations and the business world to help shape programs. The most notable was Robert Eberle, an IBM loaned executive who initiated the transformation of the IBM Education Executive Program into a Center for Educational Leadership. William Langenstein also served as an IBM loaned executive, which gave the Center a strong sense of continuity. Amie Knox and Caroline Wilson showed faith in our fledgling partnership by making it a key site for the Woodrow Wilson Institutes. Our primary donor, American Can Company (now Primerica) had leaders of exceptional vision—William Woodside, chief executive officer, and Peter Goldberg, vice-president of the foundation—who became colleagues in this partnership and our best supporters. Secondary donors, such as General Foods, IBM, and American Express, also showed faith in our educational partnership. I am grateful to our liaisons at those corporations—David Brush, Robert DeSio, Louis D. Robinson, and Dee Topol. Michael Usdan, who served as our evaluator from the outset, became a friend and offered invaluable insights. I am indebted to him for sharing his confidential reports to American Can Company. In the background, Richard Wing wrote most of our proposals and served as a kind of intellectual conscience for me as the partnership developed.

Government representatives have been supportive of all our efforts in developing the partnership. I am especially indebted to Henrik Dullea, director of state operations and policy management; Robert Maurer, executive deputy commissioner of education, and Saul Cohen, co-chair of the Governor's School and Business Alliance.

My administrative colleagues at the State University of New York, Purchase, have been equally helpful. Deanne Molinari was an indispensable associate at every stage of our efforts. The partnership could not have developed without the full support of Sheldon Grebstein, president of the college, who took every opportunity to give public advocacy to the effort; Nathaniel Siegel, vice-president for academic affairs, who was always ready to discuss the sensitive issue of institutionalizing the partnership into the college; and Lee Katz, vice-president of external affairs, who helped facilitate fund raising. I am also indebted to Gloria Forman, assistant dean, for formulating early budgets for the partnership and to Joan Mazzari, my secretary, for typing more drafts of our original proposal than either of us cares to remember and for helping me with the innumerable details of implementing the partnership.

Finally, my thanks to Resa Fremed, the executive director with whom I worked for three years. When all the rest of us left the conference room, she remained to implement our ideas and to administer the partnership. She did so with intelligence, imagination, and efficiency. Resa was later replaced by Sidney Trubowitz, who has brought our collaboration to its second stage of development.

The book itself has benefited from the perceptive suggestions of its reviewers, Kenneth E. Eble of the University of Utah and Robert E. Young of the University of Wisconsin Center, Menasha. My wife Selma, as always, has been my best and closest adviser.

T. L. G.

To my colleagues
who created and nurtured
the SUNY Purchase Westchester School Partnership

The Author

Theodore L. Gross received his B.A. degree in English (1952) from the University of Maine and his M.A. and Ph.D. degrees in English and Comparative Literature (1957, 1960) from Columbia University with highest honors. He has published fourteen books and numerous articles in professional journals on American literature and education. His major publications include *Dark Symphony: Negro Literature in America* (1968), *The Heroic Ideal in American Literature* (1971), *America in Literature* (1978), and *Academic Turmoil: The Reality and Promise of Open Education* (1980).

From 1958 to 1978, Gross worked at the City College of New York as a faculty member and administrator. In 1964–65 and 1968–69, he was a Fulbright and visiting professor at the University of Nancy, France. He has lectured widely in Asia, Europe, and Africa; he was keynote speaker at the Kyoto American Studies Seminar in 1976; and, in 1982, he was chairman of the session on "Contemporary American Literature" at the Salzburg Seminar in American Studies.

During the past twenty years, Gross has served in a variety of administrative posts: chairman of the English department, dean of humanities, and vice-president for institutional advancement at the City College of New York (1970–1978); provost and dean at the Pennsylvania State University, Capitol Campus

(1979–1983); and dean of letters and science at the State University of New York, Purchase (1983–1988). In addition, Gross has served as chairperson of the steering committee of the SUNY Purchase Westchester School Partnership, a collaboration among the university, twenty-eight school districts, Primerica and other corporations, and the local community. As of September 1988, Gross holds the position of president of Roosevelt University in Chicago.

Gross has been an active leader of a number of national organizations, including the National Council of Teachers of English, the Association of Departments of English, and the American Association of State Colleges and Universities.

Partners in Education

1

Origins and Goals
of Educational Partnerships

A history of collaborations between colleges and secondary schools in American education would be very brief indeed. Before the Second World War, only teacher-training institutions concerned themselves with the continuum of education, and they were isolated from colleges of liberal arts and sciences. Faculties offered a liberal arts curriculum to a middle-class population that was academically prepared to meet its expectations and, for the most part, homogeneous in its background. After the war, however, several cultural forces coalesced to change this landscape of learning and to lay a foundation for educational partnerships between schools and colleges.

The most striking catalyst for change occurred in 1957, when the Russians sent Sputnik, the first satellite, into space. The nation was at risk, our leaders warned, and Congress rushed to provide aid to educational programs. Academic standards were raised, great emphasis was placed on the study of mathematics and science, and there was widespread recognition that technological and political supremacy depended directly on the condition of the nation's schools and colleges. But federal support waned during the ensuing decades. It was not until the National Commission on Excellence published *A Nation at Risk* (1983) that a national movement of educational reform truly took root.

1

During this same postwar period, American education found itself moving in two fundamentally different directions. Neither of these directions mandated partnerships but both set the stage for their possibility. The development of community colleges satisfied a desire that neither high schools nor colleges met—the call for career preparation. They also proved attractive because they were within commuting distance of students, and their purpose was explicitly to serve their communities.

At the same time, major universities strengthened their research programs in response to the need for more knowledge in military, medical, and social areas. Graduate education grew increasingly significant, and it encouraged an emphasis on disciplines rather than on general education, on research and scholarship rather than on teaching. This tendency toward an academic hierarchy of values further separated the levels of education and caused college teachers, whose primary obligation was in the classroom, to perpetuate and institutionalize the graduate school paradigm and to regard precollege teaching with indifference. It also encouraged a proliferation of electives so that the curriculum became further atomized. High schools followed the lead of colleges until both levels, still separated, allowed courses to reflect the momentary interests of faculty and to lose whatever coherence they may previously have had.

By the 1970s, the contrasting roles of community colleges and graduate universities, together with a curriculum of electives that responded to social conditions, had had so significant an impact on higher education that many colleges and universities were forced to begin a review of their curricula. The faculties of four-year colleges increasingly saw the need to concern themselves with proficiencies and skills and to confront the generally low quality of high school preparation. A group of selective Pennsylvania colleges, for example, issued a document that clearly indicated their expectations of high school students. Soon institutions published core curricula that sent signals to high school educators—signals that had been largely absent in the period from 1945 to 1980. Faculties had always been dissatisfied with the academic preparation of their students, but now they confronted a reality, dramatized by educational policies that encour-

aged all students to attend college and that examined closely
the quality of their work. Students were not as well prepared
academically, and as colleges sought to meet their needs in basic
writing and mathematics, the traditional curriculum was inevitably diluted.

In the 1960s, the civil rights movement, student rebellions
throughout educational institutions, and the emphasis on career
education encouraged by the growing number of community
colleges had led to greatly expanded entering student classes,
open admissions in many urban colleges, and the need for remedial instruction in writing and mathematics. The full democratization of higher education had changed the fundamental
condition of many colleges. The initial reaction of faculty who
had dealt with a more selective student body was to resist com-
pensatory work and to place the blame on earlier levels of education. But an increased awareness of deteriorating social conditions, especially in the inner cities, made them more sympathetic
to the reasons for students' lack of preparation. Reluctantly,
college faculty expanded their programs in remediation and
English as a second language. As they assumed many of the
tasks of the high schools, they came to understand these institutions better and to work more closely with high school teachers.
At some colleges, summer programs served as bridges between
high school and college work; at others, there were conferences
that emphasized the need for an educational continuum. The
National Council Teachers of English, the Association of Departments of English, and other national organizations sponsored
workshops at their annual meetings that called for articulation
between colleges and schools. In time, collaborations emerged—
for example, the LaGuardia Community College's intermediate
school, the partnership of Queens College and Louis Armstrong
Junior High School, and others. At the other end of the spectrum, the College Board intensified its Advanced Placement
Program, Syracuse University initiated its Project Advance, and
the National Humanities Faculty expanded considerably—all
in response to high school students who wanted accelerated
learning.

Collaborations between colleges and schools did not really

4 Partners in Education

become a national movement until colleges began to suffer a
decline in enrollment in the late seventies. Demographic pro-
jections suggested that minorities and adults would dominate
the growing sectors of the student population and that the traditional college population would diminish. As a result of the need
to recruit more students, administrators urged admissions officers, as well as their faculties, to concentrate on collaborations
with the schools, and a movement toward such collaborations
began to assume a focus and an energy that it had not had before.
Educational partnerships have developed in at least four broad
directions:

The first involves alliances that concentrate on students
and their development through the academic disciplines. The
College Board's Advanced Placement Program, Syracuse University's Project Advance, and the Johns Hopkins Center for
the Advancement of Academically Talented Youth are some of
the more successful examples.

More recently, great emphasis has been placed on training teachers. Of considerable importance here have been the
Bay Area Writing Project at the University of California, Berkeley, which has become the National Writing Project; the
Academic Alliance Movement at the University of Pennsylvania;
the National Humanities Faculty, which is now the National
Faculty; the Woodrow Wilson National Fellowship Foundation
Program; and the Center for Educational Renewal at the University of Washington. These programs have gone far in creating
teacher-training partnerships.

A third group of programs has grown out of local concerns and has gained the support of community leaders. The
Boston Compact, the Yale–New Haven Teachers Institute, and
Cities in Schools—which began in Harlem and has now spread
to many other cities—illustrate this important dimension of
partnerships.

Finally, there is the kind of partnership with which I have
been associated that attempts to gather support from colleges,
schools, corporations, communities, and governmental agencies,
and places colleges at the center of the collaboration. I will be
arguing throughout these chapters that colleges and universities

should view this model as a new obligation and a new opportunity—a dimension that should become a permanent part of their institutional lives.

The number of partnerships has grown so great that the temptation is to catalogue them. That has been accomplished somewhat—initially by Maeroff in his pioneering monograph, *School and College Partnerships in Education* (1983), and more recently by Wilbur, Lambert, and Young in *The National Directory of School-College Partnerships: Current Models and Practices* (1987). This directory lists over 1,000 partnerships between schools and colleges and provides complete descriptive abstracts (300 to 500 words) on over 150 notable examples; it is "one outcome of the National Survey of School-College Partnerships, a comprehensive attempt to identify many of the collaborative programs currently in existence" (Wilbur, 1987, p. 7). Beyond the generic types that I describe briefly below, I have presented an annotated list of the more successful partnerships in Appendix A. My main purpose, however, is to identify those elements in educational collaborations that contribute to permanent partnerships and those programs that seem to work best for schools and colleges. As Goodlad (1986) has pointed out in his description of a new project involving twelve partnerships, effective institutional change is the critical measure of any successful educational collaboration. I have come to feel that colleges and universities must be the hub in the educational wheel if any long-term and permanent change is to take place. But before one can suggest a new or different model, those that have already proven to be effective must set the historical context.

Academic Disciplines

The most pervasive and influential program for accelerating students into college work has been the Advanced Placement Program. Begun in 1956 by twelve colleges and twelve high schools, it allows students to study college-level courses in their own schools and take standard, national examinations that are prepared by the Educational Testing Service under the sponsorship of the College Board. These examinations are scored

on a rising scale of achievement from one to five, and the results
are sent to those colleges that the students plan to attend. The
colleges themselves then determine whether the students are to
be advanced to higher levels of instruction.

Advanced placement has been institutionalized in American education and has, for the most part, proved to be successful.
About 29 percent of secondary schools participate nationwide,
serving 16 percent of their college-bound students. It is one of
the few programs that bridge college and high school work without threatening the schools, and it has had a tonic effect on other
courses in the curriculum. Advanced placement sets a standard
of excellence to which even less than brilliant students can aspire.
As Hanson remarks in a review of the program, "Repeated
studies—most recently from Indiana University, Harvard, and
Duke—have shown that [advanced placement] students, if placed
ahead, do indeed outperform other college students, including
those sophomores, when so identified, with similar SAT scores,
who completed their freshman courses at college rather than in
[advanced placement] schools. Further, [advanced placement]
students are more likely to persist in college, to graduate with
honors, and to take extra courses, even if they matriculate with
credits already earned. Happy learners, they are eminently pleasant to have around" (1980, p. 8).

Educational partnerships should provide a strong supporting structure for the future of the Advanced Placement Program.
Whereas a high school with only 300 students cannot afford to
offer advanced placement physics to the few students who may
want it, a consortium of schools will provide a large enough
number of students to justify a class that can be held on the
neutral grounds of a college. An incidental benefit to participating teachers is the reinforcement that comes from working with
their counterparts in other schools and interacting with college
faculty; for, as we will see in describing teacher-training programs, one of the more serious problems confronting all teachers
is their isolation in individual schools. A partnership faculty of
advanced placement teachers can counteract that tendency.

Project Advance, sponsored by Syracuse University, is
a variation of advanced placement. It also allows students to

take college-level courses—in biology, English, sociology, and mathematics—and guarantees credit at Syracuse University. Syracuse provides a transcript for other colleges, and now, after fourteen years, the program is so well established that virtually every college to which students apply will accept the credit. Eighty-seven high schools in New York, New Jersey, Massachusetts, and Michigan participate in Project Advance, offering their courses primarily to seniors who have completed all the preliminary work in the disciplines. The high school teachers, who conduct these courses in their own schools, are carefully selected and possess graduate credentials and teaching experience sufficient to allow them to offer the same courses on a college campus. Indeed, the Project Advance teachers meet each semester with Syracuse University faculty in the same disciplines, as well as for a week to fifteen days in the summer at the university. In this way, their own work is reinforced and they are able to share problems with colleagues and, most importantly, with college faculty.

In the fourteen years of its existence, Project Advance has proven to be remarkably successful. More than 42,000 students have been admitted to the program since its inception. Of equal significance has been the development of curricular materials. They reveal a program that has reached a remarkable level of maturity and sophistication.

The Johns Hopkins Center for the Advancement of Academically Talented Youth was initiated by Julian C. Stanley, a professor of psychology at the university who wanted to establish a course of study that would match the abilities of gifted mathematics students. His work led to the Study of Mathematically Precocious Youth, a program that identifies particularly gifted youngsters in the seventh grade through the Scholastic Aptitude Test in mathematics. A parallel program for Verbally Gifted Youth is now available for thirteen-year-olds interested in humanistic studies. The current director of the program is William G. Durden.

The academic programs in the Center for the Advancement of Academically Talented Youth are based on three premises (Johns Hopkins University, 1986, p. 3):

1. Academically talented students should be provided with the opportunity to learn subject matter at a pace and level geared to their abilities and developed skills rather than their age or grade level.
2. Academically talented students require a rigorous, challenging course of studies in traditional disciplines and fields of study.
3. Students' academic accomplishments should be acknowledged and certified to the extent possible, both for the students' sense of achievement and for credit or appropriate placement if desired. This may be obtained through the students' regular schools or programs such as the College Board's Advanced Placement Program.

Johns Hopkins offers its summer programs at the home campus and allows students to move through the curriculum at their own pace. It now has satellite centers at Dickinson and Franklin and Marshall colleges in Carlisle and Lancaster, Pennsylvania; at Skidmore College in Saratoga Springs, New York; and at Scripps College in Claremont, California. During the academic year, Johns Hopkins has a Saturday program at centers in various states as well as on the Baltimore campus. The results have been extraordinary. Students in foreign languages, writing, and computer science have scored at least as well as freshmen taking similar courses at Johns Hopkins. Indeed, if there is any resistance to this program, it stems from some teachers who refuse to believe that any student can accelerate so rapidly outside of the conventional classroom.

Other programs have developed at colleges and high schools that provide stimulation for gifted students. The Westinghouse Talent Search in the sciences is now established at many high schools. City College has a "Select Program in Science and Engineering for 480 tenth graders from sixteen New York City high schools . . . on the campus for twelve Saturdays each semester, providing laboratory experiences, mathematics lectures by scientists, and career counseling" (Maeroff, 1983, p. 64). Columbia University has a successful Science Honors Program. The University of California, Berkeley, offers an Accelerated High School program in which students can earn up to ten credits. The Westchester School Partnership at the State University of New York (SUNY), Purchase, has a similar program—the Young Purchase Scholars—that brings students, nominated by their district superintendent, into its eight-credit freshman great books course, "Revolutions in Western Thought." Those credits can give the student advanced standing at SUNY Purchase or be applied to other colleges. This accelerated student program is part of a broader college-school partnership, as we will see in Chapter Three.

In the development of collaborations between colleges and secondary schools, programs for gifted and talented students have led the way—partially as recruitment efforts for colleges but also as attempts to go beyond school systems that, because of financial restrictions, cannot provide sufficient advanced work for their most brilliant students. They have proved to be the easiest and most natural form of articulation since they find favor with both parents and college administrators. But they face difficulties as high school and college enrollments diminish. Schools have always been reluctant to release their finest students to accelerated programs that are extrinsic to their own educational settings. Teachers lose the pleasure of guiding gifted youngsters, the school environment itself suffers because of the absence of those standards that bright students set for their peers, and the students themselves may not have the emotional maturity to match their intellectual precocity.

One striking example of how difficult it has become to create special programs for the gifted and talented is found in Governor Mario Cuomo's attempt to establish statewide regional high schools of excellence in New York. Having earmarked seed money that allowed local Boards of Cooperative Educational Services (BOCES) to formulate plans for half- and full-day programs, he met such extreme resistance from superintendents that the program has had difficulty going forward.

Teacher-Training Partnerships

Partnerships of this kind have been slow to develop. Indeed, the entire burden of developing teachers has been left to schools of education, and there has been relatively little profes-

sional interaction between college faculty and their school counterparts through the initiative of liberal arts colleges.

One of the most prominent and certainly most successful
efforts at teacher training has been the Bay Area Writing Project, initiated by James Gray of the School of Education at Berkeley in 1973 and still coordinated by him (it is now called the
National Writing Project). Gray and his associates have described
the program well (*National Writing Project,* 1987, p. 2):

"Over the past ten years the National Writing Project has
become the major program addressing the critical need of improving the quality of teaching and writing and the quality of
student writing in the nation's classrooms. Currently [in 1987],
over 70,000 teachers are trained each year in NWP-sponsored
university and school programs. Through funding from the National Endowment for the Humanities and the Carnegie Corporation of New York, the National Writing Project has developed into an expanding network that now numbers 161 university-based sites in forty-six states, Canada, England, and Aus-
tralia, with additional sites overseas serving teachers and students
in the Department of Defense dependents' schools and in U.S.
independent schools.

The project has certain basic assumptions:

1. The writing problem affects both the universities and the
    schools. This common problem can best be solved through
    cooperatively planned university-school programs.
2. Student writing can be improved by improving the teaching
    of writing, and the best teacher of teachers is another
    teacher.
3. Change can best be accomplished by those who work in
    the schools, not by transient consultants who briefly ap-
    pear, never to be seen again, and not by packets of teacher-
    proof materials.
4. Programs designed to improve the teaching of writing
    should involve teachers at all grade levels and from all sub-
    ject areas.
5. Classroom practice and research have generated a substan-
    tial body of knowledge on the teaching of writing.
6. The intuitions of teachers can be a productive guide for field-

based research, and practicing teachers can conduct useful studies in their classrooms.

7.   Teachers of writing must write themselves.''

Leaders of the National Writing Project recognize that knowledge of a subject does not necessarily mean the ability to teach it, and they therefore concentrate on staff rather than curriculum development. They also emphasize follow-up during the academic year and conduct ''ten three-hour workshops on the teaching of writing at individual schools and districts'' for a fee of $3,000. The entire project depends heavily on ''university and community college faculty members and elementary and secondary school teachers [working] together as colleagues and partners'' (*National Writing Project,* 1987, p. 2).

The structure and procedures of the program are clear. There is a five-week invitational summer institute at which the participants are paid stipends of $500 for tuition, books, and incidental expenses. ''The aims of the institute are simple: to provide teachers with a setting in which they can share classroom successes, to make teachers more conscious of the grounds of their own teaching and to help them broaden those grounds, to give teachers an opportunity to commit themselves intensely and reflectively to writing, and finally to identify and train a corps of master classroom teachers who can effectively teach other teachers the techniques and processes of teaching writing'' (Gray, 1986, p. 39). The selection process is critical, for there is the attempt ''to identify not only teachers who have had success with writing in their own classrooms but also those who can be equally effective as teachers of other teachers'' (Gray, 1986, p. 39). At the institutes, summer fellows write and revise five major papers and work with their colleagues in small editing-response groups. The success of the program, Gray emphasizes, rests on the project's basic assumptions, which have remained unchanged over the past thirteen years. It is interesting to note how deeply dependent they are on partnership:

> The following five points are central in planning any effective school-university program. First, the idea of partnership must be believed. It is not a label

but an operating principle. School and university teachers, as colleagues, work together to determine program policy and plan program activities. A leading classroom teacher, respected by other teachers in the area, is appointed codirector and given major administrative and program responsibilities. The cooperating schools and school districts in the area share a portion of the costs of the program. Second, there must be early and mutual recognition of the knowledge that teachers at both levels can contribute to the program, and both worlds of knowledge must be tapped. Third, if special summer institutes are planned, they must be planned to include follow-up programs that maintain the working ties already established with the summer participants and make it possible for the summer participants to share their knowledge with other teachers. Fourth, any workshops that the program sponsors in the schools must be offered as voluntary programs. Even when schools contribute released time for such programs, there should be some possibility of choice offered to teachers. Last and most important, the school-university cooperative programs must be planned as success models that put a premium on what is working rather than as deficit models that treat classroom teachers as diseased, damaged, and needing repair. The Bay Area Writing Project has worked because it celebrates good teachers and good teaching [Gray, 1986, p. 45].

The National Faculty, which was founded in 1968 as the National Humanities Faculty, was originally funded for $6 million by the National Endowment for the Humanities. By now, it is a major resource for high school teachers and one of the most distinguished and productive examples of college-school collaborations. The program includes more than 700 college and university faculty who work with local teachers to improve the quality of their teaching and to help them in shaping their curricula. Directed by Benjamin Ladner, with offices at Emory University, the National Faculty encounter the actualities of public school teaching directly by working "in the schools with groups of teachers who are committed to reading, writing, discussing, and developing better thinking abilities. Outstanding college professors in English, history, science, art, mathematics, and foreign languages are appointed to the National Faculty to work with school teachers. They teach them more about their subjects; they help them work together as intellectual colleagues; and they make them more effective teachers, here and now" (*National Faculty*, 1987, p. 2).

According to Donald Bigelow, senior administrator of the program, the National Faculty has three primary characteristics. The first involves a two-year plan that a group of teachers or project team in a school must design; this plan determines what kind of humanities faculty member will be chosen to join the team. Second, the National Faculty member visits the school for two days in both winter and spring. During the spring session, a core group of National Faculty and teachers plan for a two- or three-week summer program that will typically involve thirty to forty participants. The third dimension of the program involves follow-up and institutionalization within the school, which will require administrators to provide released time and resources essential for the plan to succeed. In each case a principal or assistant principal serves as the project administrator and a teacher becomes the academic coordinator. When the project is in its planning phase, other college faculty located near the school district are invited by the National Faculty to join the group to provide further assistance.

Funding for the National Faculty stems from private foundations, national agencies, and local businesses. It now includes more than 600 projects. In the past, these efforts have been extremely varied:

> There has been a program to teach grammar and writing at a school in the mountains of West Virginia by using the region's folklore, music, and

history. Another program in a typical small industrial town in Indiana led to teaching literature and history by having students interview their parents and grandparents about the impact of the Depression and then supplement the interview with appropriate readings. Benjamin DeMott, Andrew W. Mellon professor of the humanities at Amherst College, is among the better known members of the National Humanities Faculty. He has found the experience very similar to being a member of a curriculum committee at his own college—full of the same politics and intrigue. In other words, faculty life in a junior high school or a high school is not necessarily any freer of personality clashes than in higher education. What this means, DeMott has discovered, is that professors who agree to help their precollegiate colleagues should not approach the task with naiveté.

"Once you are there," DeMott observes, "you may say you are just a visitor, but you are into it up to your ears and you are seen as an ally of the teacher who arranged to bring you to the school. You have to figure out how to enlarge the team and start building bridges immediately. Once they trust you, you are treated with warmth and you get a sense of common enterprise. When you do something like this, you get to know more about where your students come from" [Maeroff, 1983, pp. 34–35].

One of the major programs of the National Faculty is currently being conducted in the Atlanta school system. It is funded by the Rockefeller Foundation and local businesses.

At the University of Pennsylvania, the Academic Alliance Movement: School-College Faculty Collaboration has been gathering momentum under the guidance of Claire Gaudiani. Established in 1982, it has many of the same characteristics as the programs developed by the National Humanities Faculty.

It encourages voluntary "alliances of working professionals" who forge "local communities of inquiry into the disciplines" (Gaudiani and Burnett, 1986, p. 1).

The Academic Alliance Movement rests on assumptions that suggest a commonality between school "teachers" and college "faculty"—a convergence in which the two groups are often engaged in the same work. More than 50 percent of teachers now have at least master's degrees, and there is constant pressure through in-service courses to develop knowledge within the disciplines. At the same time, college faculty must attend more than ever to remedial English and mathematics and to other subjects normally taught in high schools. They teach an increasingly heterogeneous group of students, and few publish regularly (indeed, fewer than 40 percent have published anything in the last two years). They belong to unions just as teachers do; and women, who tended to dominate precollegiate teaching, have now joined college faculties in greater numbers. The old saws that "teachers teach students and faculty teach subjects," that "high school teachers have baccalaureate degrees and professors have Ph.D.'s," or that teachers are engaged only in teaching whereas faculty pursue research as well as teach are no longer entirely accurate; there has clearly been a conflation of interests and proficiencies. The common characteristics that teachers and faculty share have been shaped largely by the democratization of higher education and by an information society whose occupations demand higher levels of literacy and computational skills, as well as broader knowledge. "American education is unique," Rickover has observed. "Where else is algebra taught in elementary school and remedial reading in college?" (DiGennaro, 1985, p. 5) Clearly these trends will intensify in the future and form a massive foundation for partnerships between schools and colleges.

The Academic Alliance Movement has ninety-four collaborative groups in foreign languages and literature and is developing alliances—currently eleven—in history, English, international studies, mathematics, and science. This movement is largely a response to the changing cultures of schools and colleges and concentrates on bringing together teachers in common disciplines within local communities. In the strict sense, academic alliances, each of which includes twelve to sixty members, are not institutionally based, as are college-school partnerships. Instead, they ask teachers and faculty to treat each other as equals in a kind of disciplinary renewal. There is heavy stress on equality, and college faculty are constantly urged not to flaunt their professional titles and not to try to dominate meetings. A favorite image in the description of the program is that of two buses carrying passengers who have had institutional differences that have blocked "the faculty aboard each bus from finding each other. Alliances arrange a common time each month when faculty *get off their buses,* and go to the park—the common ground—where they meet each other to reflect on the field from an adult perspective. Once on common ground, it becomes less significant what bus a teacher came on, and more significant what contribution he or she can make to the community of inquiry in the discipline" (Gaudiani and Burnett, 1986, p. 8).

The concentration on bringing teachers at different levels of education together makes the Academic Alliance Movement particularly compelling, and it does seem to have been remarkably successful—in its five-year history more than seventy alliance groups have been formed. But the stress on equality seems to be unnecessarily defensive. There is no question that the main reasons for the slow development of partnerships between colleges and schools has been the reluctance of liberal arts faculty to participate, their isolation from schools of education and from the secondary schools that send them their students, and their tendency to be patronizing to teachers. But after one has deplored the unfortunate divisions between colleges and schools and the culpability that colleges must bear, one must acknowledge that there are fundamental differences between the cultures of high schools and colleges. While it is essential to reinforce the professionalism of teaching, there will always be certain necessary and healthy differences between schools and colleges because of the age differences in the students, because pedagogy is more important in teaching younger students, and because college teachers need to have a deeper knowledge of their subject matter, just as elementary and secondary schoolteachers need to have a keener understanding of human behavior and instructional strategies. This is one reason why the Advanced Placement Program, Project Advance, the National Faculty, and the National Writing Project are so attractive: they respect the differences between school and college teachers and capitalize on them.

A new model for teaching training that has developed rapidly since 1982 and is particularly compatible with the kind of educational partnership that is centered at a college and reaches out to schools, corporations, communities, and governmental agencies. Called the Woodrow Wilson National Fellowship Foundation Program and based at Princeton University, it depends upon high school peer teaching, which is buttressed by the support and cooperation of a college faculty. Master teachers are selected nationally and brought to Princeton University where they are brought up to date on curriculum development within a specific discipline. Then groups of four are formed and go into the field, usually a college campus, to teach their peers in one-week mini-institutes that are arranged by local faculty. The Woodrow Wilson program has concentrated upon math and science, but the model can be adapted to the humanities, social sciences, and the arts as well and thus become the centerpiece for a whole range of activities. The program and its possibilities are described at length in Chapter Seven.

One of the most elaborate and ambitious college-school collaborations that reaches beyond teacher training has been initiated by John Goodlad. This National Network for Educational Renewal, is headquartered at the University of Washington, with initial funding from the Exxon Education and Danforth foundations. Goodlad and his colleagues are concentrating on "the education of educators" and seeking ways to improve it. His five-year program focuses on three interrelated areas: (1) "a study of 1,300 schools, colleges, and departments of education in the nation to determine the current conditions surrounding the education of educators"; (2) "an examination of the preparation programs of other professions such as medicine, law, engineering, architecture, and the arts . . . to determine those practices—both past and present—that might lead to a better under-

standing of new ways to develop models of educator preparation''; and (3) ''the development of some twelve [now thirteen]
partnerships of school districts and universities, each with a focus
on the simultaneous improvement of both preparation and practice, and the development of a national network to link these
partnerships in common research and school improvement efforts'' (Cordovea, 1986, pp. 1, 2).

　　As Goodlad points out, such partnerships are critical
because ''improvement of public schooling and improvement
of the ways in which educators are prepared to go hand in hand''
(Cordovea, 1986, p. 1). Better schools depend upon better-
trained educators, but a key element of an improved training
program is the creation of exemplary school-based training sites
in which prospective educators can observe, learn, and practice good techniques. ''We must lessen the gulf between higher
education and the schools,'' Goodlad contends, ''but at the same
time we must recognize that both must be improved. Partnerships between school districts and nearby institutions of higher
education will seek mutual improvement'' (Cordovea, 1986, p.
2). Thirteen local partnerships—in Arizona, Arkansas, Colorado, Hawaii, Indiana, Maine, Massachusetts, Michigan, New
York, Utah, Virginia, Washington State, and Wyoming—have
made a five-year commitment to the national network, which
includes ''a newsletter, consultants, periodic national meetings
of the partnerships' executive directors, and the creation of six
or seven national task forces on specific reform topics'' (Olson,
1986, p. 16). The individual partnerships must be financially
self-supporting and their concerns will develop from local needs.
Each partnership has the endorsement and support of the university's chief executive officer, so that involvement goes beyond
the school or college of education and decision making can be
made at the highest level of each institution. Each partnership
will serve as a case study of the change process and document
its successes and failures for other network members. Goodlad
believes that current reform legislation consists ''primarily of
adding 'more of the same' to schools, in the form of more time,
more homework, more 'basics,' more standards, and more accountability'' (Olson, 1986, p. 16). What is needed is ''nothing

short of fundamental reviews of educational programs for both children and youth, on the one hand, and those who teach and administer them, on the other" (Olson, 1986, p.16).

Goodlad's efforts are based on certain premises. A successful partnership "is in large measure *symbiotic* . . . it unites unlike entities rather intimately in mutually beneficial relationships," and it has certain fundamental characteristics: "The partners are to some degree dissimilar. The goal is mutual satisfaction of self-interests. Each party is selfless enough to assure this mutual satisfaction of self-interests" (Olson, 1986, p. 16). The National Network for Educational Renewal, once it has tested these formulations within the next five years, will go far in establishing the credibility and importance of educational partnerships.

Partnerships for Communities

Another kind of partnership has responded to community needs. Because they enjoy local support, these are often the most successful enterprises. The efforts to set national standards for teachers, as formulated in *A Nation Prepared,* and the statewide regulations that have driven the recent reform movement concentrate on excellence and set goals for the society at large. But they often avoid more difficult issues—the needs of underprivileged and underprepared urban children and school dropouts, for example—that continue to resist solution as they grow more intense. Because of immediate pressure, these issues are more likely to be addressed locally. Seeley (1985) takes the argument even further and makes a most compelling case that unless we involve community groups, no standards or regulations will have much effect. This in turn may mean making significant compromises that traditionalists are generally unwilling to consider.

A list of community-based educational partnerships would comprise a book itself—I have included some of the more prominent ones in Appendix A. They exist in many communities throughout the country and testify to the growing significance of this movement. Two of the more dramatic examples have developed in New Haven and Boston.

In 1978, Yale University organized the Yale–New Haven Teachers Institute in conjunction with the local school system. This institute conducts seminars in a broad range of liberal arts subjects for approximately eighty teachers in the high schools. They take place from March to July and involve curriculum development as well as continuing education for the teachers. Funded by the National Endowment for the Humanities, the institute has been able to pay teachers a $650 stipend. It has also opened university facilities to them and allowed them a professional life they would not otherwise have. So successful has the program been in the New Haven schools that fifty city businesses have subsequently provided supporting funds. Yale itself is engaged in an endowment campaign to raise $4 million so that the program can be permanently established. As James R. Vivian, director of the program, has pointed out, this institute and college-school collaborations like it will flourish because of a declining student population and a teaching corps in which there will be little turnover. Indeed, he stresses that it is more important to assist current teachers than recruit new ones.

The seminars of the Yale–New Haven Teachers Institute are varied. In 1987 they included "Science, Technology, and Society"; "Human Nature, Biology, and Social Structure"; "Epic, Romance, and the American Dream"; and "Writing About American Culture." Participants prepared reading lists and a curriculum unit under the supervision of Yale professors. The units were published as a book and distributed to New Haven teachers.

Michael G. Cook, professor of English at Yale, has noted that the seminars focus on the traditional roles of teachers and college faculty—the former tends to concentrate on the student and the latter on the subject. They are also a response to the separate career paths of the college professor and the high school teacher. The seminars underscore how much university people can learn about learning and how much high school teachers can deepen their disciplinary knowledge. The process provides still another example of what participants in the Academic Alliance Movement are learning—college faculty and school teachers are no longer so dissimilar.

There is, of course, an unspoken question behind the
Yale–New Haven Teachers Institute. What happens to teachers
who are fearful of professors who may be teaching highly selective, extremely bright students at Yale—students who may in
fact be more engaging than the teachers? The danger of losing
less well-prepared teachers is real and not fully answered by the
institutes. One way of helping those who tend to be ignored is
through a program such as the one devoted to motivation described in Chapter Five.

The desegregation plan set forth in 1976 by Federal Judge
W. Arthur Garrity, Jr., led to the establishment of an educational partnership in Boston—a city that for a time was particularly tense with racial distrust and animosity. Called the
Boston School–College Collaboration, it originally ordered the
pairing of Boston schools with colleges and universities to improve educational programs in a school system that now includes
more than 56,000 elementary, middle, and high school students.
In 1975, the colleges and universities signed an agreement to
raise the college acceptance rate of Boston Public School graduates 25 percent by 1989. Services were set up that included
a college information center located at the Boston Public Library;
a scholarship program called ACCESS for low-income students;
and an association of six high schools and seventeen colleges
called the Fenway Retention Consortium that "focuses on how
colleges can recruit, enroll, and *retain* students who are graduated
from Boston high schools" (Maeroff, 1983, p. 11). The collaboration has raised a $3.8 million endowment to support the
partnership.

The results were mixed initially. The faculty of MIT was
particularly cooperative and helped to establish the Mario
Umana Harbor School of Science and Technology by training
teachers and working with them to equip the public high school
and design its curriculum. Other colleges were slower to participate, but in the 1983–84 school year alone it was estimated
that the colleges and universities had contributed to the Boston
school system a combination of scholarships, services, time, and
materials worth $5.6 million.

The one element that was initially missing was coordination. When Robert Spillane became superintendent of the Boston

public schools in 1981, he was informed that the existing programs lacked clear goals and a process of evaluation. Out of this need, the Boston School-College Collaboration developed, and in 1982 a permanent coordinator was appointed.

A most interesting youth program, Cities in Schools (CIS), is a direct community attempt to deal with truancy in urban centers. Begun in Harlem more than twenty years ago as the response of a religious group called Young Life to juvenile drug abuse, CIS has grown to fifty programs in fifteen cities. The basis of the program is that any resolution to school dropout problems must be holistic and that the at-risk student needs to have his self-esteem bolstered through a variety of social services—not simply education. "A partnership is needed to combat our dropout problem. No single institution created the dilemma we face today. No single institution can cure it" (Hall, 1986, p. 15). An attempt is made to develop programs small enough to be personal in milieus that are usually impersonal. "When a kid is not performing in the classroom," the assistant director of Texas programs, which reach 8,000 youngsters in seven school districts, notes, "something somewhere else in his life is going wrong" (p. 21). CIS therefore "marshals resources that include personal counselors, social agencies, clergy, volunteer groups from the Boys' Clubs to the Junior League, municipal resources such as recreation facilities and specialists, medical centers, and job trainers. By having these social services function together, the CIS staff members, trained in education or social work" (p. 21), foster communication among parents, teachers, and young people. Staffers closely watch a student's progress. Follow-up is said to be immediate if grades drop or there is absenteeism.

Students are referred to a CIS program by principals, counselors, teachers, and parents because of poor attendance, low academic achievement, disruptive behavior, or family problems; and though they continue to attend classes, they report to "a team of skilled professional counselors trained by CIS" (Hall, 1986, p. 21). CIS programs are located at school sites that are accessible to all the student participants.

CIS has had "a tortuous and somewhat circuitous history'' (Hall, 1986, p. 22), according to Douglas Johnston, national vice-president of the program. It was threatened most seriously by the Reagan administration funding cuts in the early 1980s; it now depends on local, private, and government funding and, through a curious reversal of government policy, it has secured support from the Departments of Justice, Labor, Education, and Health and Human Services. The CIS program is no longer an experiment; its headquarters is located in Washington, D.C., and successful programs exist in Atlanta; Indianapolis; Houston; New York City; Bethlehem, Pennsylvania; Los Angeles; Washington, D.C.; Columbia, South Carolina; Pottsville, Pennsylvania; Bridgeport, Connecticut; Charlotte, North Carolina; Pittsburgh; and West Palm Beach. The program proved to be so compelling to those of us who were developing the SUNY Purchase Westchester School Partnership that we secured significant funding from the General Foods Corporation to adopt it in Westchester County. A detailed account of that undertaking is given in Chapter Six.

Collaborations between colleges and schools will inevitably need the support of private business, government, and the community, but they must depend on their own efforts if they are to succeed in the long run. In this brief overview of educational partnerships, I have not included corporate programs of localized interest. Some of the more prominent collaborations include the New York City Partnership, under the former leadership of David Rockefeller, its chairman, and Frank Macchiarola, its president; the network of Join-A-School programs in New York City, originated by Joseph Califano; and the Public Education Fund of Pittsburgh, led by David Bergholz, which ''encourages business, labor, civic leadership, parents, and other concerned parties to join with the local school system'' (Bergholz, 1985, p. 1). As important as these relationships may be, I am persuaded with Goodlad that they are primarily ''helping connections toward which business usually adopts a philanthropic *noblesse oblige* attitude'' (Goodlad, 1986, p. 2). For permanent leadership, colleges and universities working with school systems must be central. In order to ensure that success, colleges and universities must become the central agents of educational partnerships—and not just their schools or programs of education, however important their role has been and will continue to be, but their colleges of liberal arts and science as well. Their faculty present the subjects that future teachers will adapt to their own needs, their administration has a development office that can organize proposals for the private sector, they have research foundations through which contributions can be channeled so that an audit trail is established, and their students can be engaged as interns and assistants for various projects. Finally, their entire structure is shaped not only to teach but to provide the administrative leadership essential for successful educational partnerships.

Although there are many types of partnerships that have met specific needs, the history of collaborations between schools and colleges has reached a watershed. They now must become more than marginal to our educational institutions, and this means that their place, at the undergraduate level, is in the college of liberal arts and sciences as well as the traditional pre-professional programs in education. For my account of partnership leaders, the intricacies of fund raising and institutionalization, and some of the major programs that can comprise a consortium, I have used as a point of reference my own collaboration—the SUNY Purchase Westchester School Partnership. Rather than write generally about these matters and offer countless examples of how they can work, I have rooted them in a model that I believe can be replicated or adapted by any college or university. This model does not represent a total solution or pretend to be the only form that partnerships should take. It is inevitably limited by geography, although in encompassing all of Westchester County—more than 10,000 teachers and 100,000 students—it is more a mirror of American society than may at first seem to be the case. It is inevitably a creation of a specific time, but as a direct response to *A Nation at Risk* (National Commission, 1983), it was born in the midst of the most important educational reform movement of the twentieth century and was able to profit from all the efforts, described in this chapter, that helped to shape that movement.

2

Organizing and Leading
Partnerships

The principle of partnership is to engage diverse constituents to improve the quality of learning. As the following brief descriptions suggest, the constituents must reflect the total community. It is important to remember that improvement of learning means strengthening elementary and secondary schooling through the creation of college-based partnerships. The hub of the wheel must be the college, the spokes of the wheel the schools. There will be many other partners, but they will be attracted to the collaboration and will be effective in their relationship to it only to the extent that the bond between the college and schools forms the permanent source of continuing support. In examining the core of that source or center, we will focus on the chief academic officer of the college, the superintendent of the school, and the executive director who must work with both of them.

Deans of Colleges

The catalyst for creating a college-school collaboration can emerge from many different sources, but usually it results from the financial support of a foundation, corporation, or state or federal agency. In most cases, the college or university activates the request and is the recipient of the gift. In some large metropolitan school systems, grant officers can initiate or respond to educational partnerships—the Boston Compact is a good example—but most collaborations have been organized and sustained by colleges and universities.

Within the college, a chief academic officer must assume authority and responsibility for the partnership and make it central to all activities. In some institutions, programs and schools of education will continue to be the professional home of any collaboration, but the national trend—most evidenced by the recent statement of the Holmes group and by the forceful arguments of Bernard Gifford (1986) and Diane Ravitch (1983)—is toward keeping the professional preparation of teachers at the graduate level, after they have acquired a traditional liberal arts education. Partnerships located in colleges of liberal arts and sciences will demand the full support of the administration, even though they can profit from graduate programs in education if the partnerships happen to be in or near universities.

Most of the successful partnerships thus far created within universities have either been associated with their schools of education, such as Project Advance and the Bay Area Writing Project, or have been developed as institutes and centers, such as the Yale–New Haven Teachers Institute and the Johns Hopkins Center for the Advancement of Academically Talented Youth. They may draw upon liberal arts faculty, but they have not been designed to make the faculty responsible for them. These models will undoubtedly be replicated and will serve a significant purpose. But until educational partnerships are at the center of the academic enterprise—and that can happen only when colleges of liberal arts and sciences choose to own them—faculties at different levels of education will not really be speaking with each other and the college-school collaborations will be as vulnerable as any other specially funded program.

I do not minimize the difficulty of persuading traditional faculty that working with elementary and high school educators and pursuing research projects that may result from interaction with them can be as rewarding and meaningful as other forms of scholarship, but I am encouraged by the increasing number of faculty members who willingly become involved in general education and those who have regarded remediation in

English and mathematics with as much enthusiasm and imagination as they have teaching in their own disciplines. It is also
clear that federal and state funding agencies such as the National Science Foundation and the National Endowment for the
Humanities have developed categories that bridge the school
and college cultures and that have already elicited a response
from college faculty. National organizations such as the national
councils of Teachers of English and of Mathematics and the
American Association for Higher Education have followed a similar pattern. Most importantly, college administrators know that
the very nature of the curriculum depends upon who is coming
through the system and that finally, as Hodgkinson (1985) reminds us, it is all one system. In David Saxon's farewell address as president of the University of California, he explicitly
warned everyone in the California system that by the year 2000
"California is likely to become the first state in the nation whose
population is made up predominantly of members of minority
groups. . . . Intelligent self-interest, the welfare of the nation,
and justice all demand that we do something to make sure that
the young people of the state are qualified for education at the
University of California" (Hodgkinson, 1987). Saxon saw that
if concrete plans for coordination between colleges and schools
were not developed, California would face serious educational
and economic problems. He also recognized that it will not be
only the minority children who are in trouble, it will be the
university itself (Hodgkinson, 1987). Educational partnerships
can no longer be marginal activities if colleges and universities
are serious about their future. These partnerships belong in colleges of liberal arts and sciences.

Once the partnership has been anchored in liberal arts
and sciences, the dean assumes a critical role. His or her belief
in the importance of articulation with earlier levels of education will influence both administrative associates and faculty
members by making participation in the partnership part of the
rewards system of the college. It is critical to reiterate to faculty
that participation is voluntary and that they must continue to
pursue research and teaching as always. But as the partnership
takes shape, its benefits will become clear to them: the excite-

ment of working directly with highly motivated teachers and administrators; recruitment advantages, as scores of classroom teachers come to the campus, meet faculty, and return to their students; the supplementary income that an underpaid faculty needs; and the research, especially in the social sciences, that can result from interaction with the schools.

Partnership activities may be initially resisted by a college faculty for a variety of reasons. Some may feel unqualified to deal with the pedagogical problems of schools; others will claim it is not their mandate; still others will charge that resources are being drawn from the more legitimate activities of the college. It would be imprudent to require faculty members to participate in college-school activities. Once the partnership becomes an organic unit of the college, however, participation should be accepted as a valid professional activity in support of promotion and tenure. As it is woven into the administrative texture of the campus and its benefits become more manifest, the partnership will be accepted and work its change on the entire college community.

The dean is in the best position to affect that institutional change. As Morris points out, a dean "is the highest officer in the hierarchy expected to have regular, operational contact with the faculty, the deliverers of the university's service. This close, everyday association with the central element of the institution's personnel puts the dean at the center of a university's raison d'être, that is, teaching and research. No higher officer enjoys this intimate proximity to the primary action of an academic institution" (1981, p. 8).

The relationship of the dean to superintendents is more precarious, for they come from two separate cultures and are accountable to two different constituencies. Since the funding for a partnership will usually come through the college, the dean will inevitably become central in developing the initial proposal and many of the later fund-raising efforts. My own experience with the SUNY Purchase Westchester School Partnership was typical. I was charged with writing the proposal that would be funded by the American Can Foundation. This meant that, together with my colleagues at Purchase, I was able to recommend the terms of the partnership—its themes, its boundaries, its possibilities—to which the superintendents and others responded. It also meant that all fund-raising activities originated in my office. In time, this fact became significant, as the prospects for fund raising grew. Whenever possible, proposals carried the participation of the eleven, presently twenty-six, school districts, as success fed on success, but the proposals were written and ultimately signed off in the dean's office. Thus, academic and fiscal controls were both clearly rooted in the dean's office. The superintendents were grateful for these centralized controls, however, because they created order in a partnership that could easily have fallen into chaos, given its many different districts dispersed throughout the county.

Indeed, the attitude of the superintendents and their relationship to me was one of the basic reasons for the success of our partnership. When we first established our steering committee of eleven superintendents and four college administrators, they elected me as chairperson—even though they scarcely knew me. As dean of the College of Liberal Arts and Sciences, I was a neutral figure among the superintendents and represented the college that had attracted the funding. But it was not simply neutrality that made the dean an obvious choice as leader or the college an ideal site and gathering place for ideas and projects. It was the prestige of the campus and the willingness of faculty to work with teachers—adults talking to adults in their own academic disciplines—that made the campus especially appealing to the superintendents. It was the automatic support of college services—a sophisticated development office, an administration promising space and time—that sustained the structure of the partnership and gave it an administrative flexibility that the superintendents found attractive.

The college was both a center and a clearinghouse—the hub of the wheel. From the outset, the superintendents expressed their satisfaction at dealing directly with a college of liberal arts and sciences. In this sense, our partnership was somewhat different from other kinds of collaborations between colleges and schools, for the disciplines dictated the authority of the educational process. The superintendents, who after all were paid to

run school districts and not a college-school collaboration, could
serve on a steering committee and assume responsibility for individual projects of particular value to them. They could boast
of activities that embellished their daily duties at no cost to their
districts except their personal time and nominal annual dues.
They could relate to me as a college administrator without fear
of competitiveness. My own success depended heavily on im-
partiality to each of the superintendents, however much I might
favor one who was particularly conscientious. And I needed to
discover ways that all of them could be drawn into active leadership of the partnership.

The hub of the educational wheel was the college of liberal
arts and sciences, and the partnership found its continuity, public
image, and academic strength there. As dean, I brought a strong
bias to the concept of partnership, especially in terms of articulation with earlier levels of education. The chairpersons of humanities, social sciences, and natural sciences as well as the faculty
within the College of Liberal Arts and Sciences, clearly felt this
bias.

SUNY Purchase is of course small. It has only 3,000 students (4,000 head count), 1,400 of whom are in the College of
Liberal Arts and Sciences. Although the role of the dean will
remain crucial even in universities with 25,000 or 30,000 students, departmental chairpersons must be willing to work with
him or her in creating relationships with the public schools. The
dean's role will be less prominent as the size of the institution
increases and disciplinary access, as the Academic Alliance
Movement has shown, is more likely to be through chairpersons
of English, foreign languages, biology, or other disciplines. The
larger the university, the greater the authority of the chairperson
or head and the more important his or her role in the rewards
system. If the chairperson joins the dean in partnership, the links
with the disciplines will be assured, and the concept of collaboration should pervade the very fabric of a college of liberal arts
and sciences.

The special relationship of the dean to school superintendents can be illustrated by my own experiences when our partnership began. In designing the first draft of the proposal, I felt
like a charlatan, for I was writing a document that involved levels

of education at which I had never taught. I was working out of a liberal arts office that scarcely had enough resources for our own college work, and I was at a campus whose faculty had little professional interest in precollegiate education. For years I had believed that liberal arts faculties had created a serious problem by refusing, on the whole, to interact with their colleagues in the schools and that the relegation of prospective teachers to professional programs at the undergraduate level was a serious error. Instinctively, I knew that teachers should be talking directly to teachers at every level of education, but I was not sure how this could be accomplished, beyond ephemeral workshops or conferences. Moreover, I was keenly aware that it would be very difficult to persuade a college faculty, committed to research and teaching for professional advancement, that the partnership should be a real concern for them. At the same time, I was aware that individual faculty members had been quietly engaged in meeting with their counterparts in the schools, that they had visited high school departments for lectures, and that schoolteachers came to campus through our continuing education classes. The challenge was to give administrative coherence to these efforts, to encourage them, and to find still more resources for collaboration.

The audacity of drafting a proposal to improve learning in schools where I had never been an educator was tempered by the fact that the ideas belonged largely to the superintendents and could be checked by them at every stage. All of them were former teachers who knew instinctively whether something would work. They formed a pragmatic, pedagogical control so that the final report to the American Can Foundation bore the imprimatur of their authority. If the administrative center resided in my office, pedagogical and educational authority belonged to the superintendents. And this relationship of respect and trust formed the foundation of the partnership.

Superintendents of Schools

Superintendents must be among the leaders of a partnership. Their authority in the schools seems absolute and carries the endorsement of the school board, the administration, and the teachers. Together with the dean and other college administrators who comprise the steering committee, they should be highly influential in selecting the partnership's major programs. Each project should have the personal advocacy and leadership of a superintendent and, if possible, grow out of his or her particular interests in education.

The partnership offers superintendents a special opportunity. Because they need to represent and impress the constituencies within their districts—school boards, administrators, teachers, parents—they can develop that imaginative, experiential program they have always wished to promote, with little to lose. Moreover, they can return to their districts as genuine educational leaders of their communities. The superintendents with whom I dealt were among the finest educators I have known: handpicked leaders of very demanding school districts that wanted to be in advance of whatever was happening nationally. And, of course, they had impeccable credentials from Columbia's Teachers College, New York University, Fordham University, the University of Chicago, and elsewhere. Buried in their backgrounds were the doctoral dissertations and incidental essays that revealed them as educational thinkers as well as putative administrators. One had done research on unmotivated students, another was keenly interested in staff development, a third knew a great deal about counseling, a fourth felt deeply about leadership training, a fifth had a passion for the arts. And on it went. The point was to synchronize these concerns with the needs of the partnership. Not surprisingly, the two matched, and the superintendents felt liberated, activated—students once again, but leaders, too.

It was clear from the outset that the only way this college-school collaboration would prosper was through the active leadership of the school superintendents. Indeed, they immediately formed a steering committee, claimed ownership of the partnership, and wanted their districts to enjoy its primary benefits. My own view was that the school districts near Purchase were not diverse enough, and at our initial meeting I urged the nine superintendents to include several larger, urban districts. The discussion was predictable. My colleagues and I at Purchase argued for heterogeneity and complexity, even for difficulty, if this partnership were to become—as American Can wanted it to be—a statewide model that would represent larger issues in microcosm. As Harold Hodgkinson (1985) and many others were pointing out, the schools were becoming increasingly populated by Hispanic, black, and Asian students—in Westchester County as elsewhere—and not to include the Yonkers and Mount Vernon districts, where these groups were a strong presence, was to be exclusive and indeed parochial.

The nine founding superintendents had already collaborated in programs with the college, they reminded us, and had devoted considerable time and effort to the foundation of the consortium. They had come forward and shown interest. Why should they reach outward now to new districts? This initial reasoning was motivated by more than self-interest. The superintendents were rightly worried about moving too fast—the unhappy fate of most partnerships—and they felt that the superintendents of larger districts had concerns that were different in kind as well as in degree from their own. Finally, they predicted that the superintendents of larger districts would not have time to participate actively. (This proved to be a specious argument; the degree of involvement by the superintendents depended on the individual and had little to do with the size of the district.)

The initial exchange was fascinating and grew warmer, as territories were staked out and the separate agendas of the college and the schools revealed themselves. At this early moment in its history, the Purchase administrators wanted to develop civic interest in and greater visibility for the partnership, attract students to the college, and extend it as a public institution—mixed but, on the whole, commendatory motives. The superintendents wanted what they could not afford on their own, a margin of excellence (as the cliché goes), an edge on the competition, so that they would please their sophisticated and demanding school boards. They did not want to be left out of any new enterprise. Some of them wanted something more, something personal—a fulfillment of themselves as educators as well as managers. These leaders had yet to realize the untested ideas of their youth; they wanted to strike out individually, call an idea their own, turn dissertation rhetoric into reality. The privately funded partnership offered this possibility, for it moved beyond the vested interests of their own school districts. All these motives gave reason for hope.

These were private agendas, but there was—and every superintendent knew it—the controlling influence of the college. The college had been invited by American Can to apply for the grant, the college would be the home of the partnership, and the college brought a prestige to schoolteachers and administrators that they openly desired. And so the college, at this formative stage and at every step in this precarious, uncharted partnership, held the rudder and steered the course and shaped significant decisions.

We settled (reluctantly, in the case of the superintendents) on Yonkers and Mount Vernon as the two additional school districts that would be invited to be founding members of the partnership—Yonkers, full of the fiscal, educational, and racial problems of an urban community; Mount Vernon, strongly represented by minorities.

The amount of authority possessed by the superintendents surprised me and made me realize, as we developed individual projects, how essential they were to the success of the partnership and how we had to insist that they not delegate their power to any associate. There are strong unions in each of the districts, and some of the union leaders have become figures of importance in various programs. But however much these leaders may legislate for higher salaries or other professional benefits and even, when provoked, be instrumental in removing an administrator, the central figure in a district is inevitably the superintendent.

Two examples will illustrate the power of the superintendent. The first significant project of our partnership was a Math/Science Institute. The State Education Department had created Math/Science and Computer Training Teacher centers in various school districts throughout New York. Within a month of the time that we had formally established the partnership and appointed the executive director, we had the opportunity to apply for funding of a Teachers Center that would be affiliated with but not controlled by the partnership. The United Federation of Teachers had successfully pressed for support of the centers, and the legislation stipulated that there was to be a majority representation of teachers on the policy board. As we assembled our teachers from each of the school districts, together with a representative parent, some SUNY Purchase administrators, faculty, and three superintendents, we looked for a leader. We found him in a superintendent—Ronald D. Valenti of the Blind Brook School District—who was particularly interested in staff development and science education. Although everyone (especially the superintendent himself) knew that his position was temporary and some union leaders had difficulties with his role because the policy board of the Teachers Center was meant to be led by teachers, the superintendent was able to guide the policy board through its organizational period. He held the board together through his sensitivity to the teachers and representatives of other groups, served as a strong connecting link between the policy board and the steering committee of the partnership, guided the Teachers Center through its first year, helped to secure renewed funding, and served as the mentor to a teacher on the policy board who became the subsequent chairperson. There is no question that the center would never have flourished without his firm, sensitive leadership. He also became a role model to teachers who had administrative aspirations themselves.

A second illustration of the superintendent as leader occurred with the establishment of the guidance counselor project. We had learned of a highly successful model sponsored by the Institute for Educational Leadership in Washington, which provided for four-week summer externships in corporations (the model and our adaptation of it are described in Chapter Eight). The early meetings of the counselors could have been confused and ultimately futile. I watched numerous representatives from eleven school districts—twenty-five in all—complain about the low status of guidance counselors, their peripheral role to administrators and teachers, their need for significant summer salaries (''who would *ever* work for $800 as a four-week summer extern in a corporation?''), and their static position in the hierarchy of the school system. The average tenure of guidance counselors in these districts was fourteen years, and they looked jaded. But the meetings were not chaotic because the superintendent—Joseph Carbone of the Harrison School District—committed himself and his district to the project. At the first meeting, moreover, he indicated his enthusiastic endorsement of the Washington model. "This is the best model I have seen in thirty years," he said, "and I began as a guidance counselor. . . . The guidance counselor should be a pivotal person, although that hasn't been sufficiently understood by superintendents and principals" (Carbone, personal communication, 1985). The superintendent framed the discussion and asserted his authority: As long as this larger group felt the enterprise was worth pursuing, he would lead the meetings until the project was launched. Throughout that academic year, a small committee designed the adaptation and secured the funding. As a last step, the superintendent had his staff and students produce and distribute a *Handbook for Career Opportunities in Westchester County*.

In recognizing the need for continuing involvement of superintendents in the practical administration of each project, we reinforced the structure of the steering committee. This committee is crucial to the success of any partnership and must be sensitively organized. As the partnership grows, the districts represented on the steering committee will need to rotate so that the committee remains small and functional and no one district feels it is left out.

Steering Committees

Inevitably, the steering committee will be composed of college administrators and school superintendents and will be responsible for all policy making in the partnership. In our case, the college representatives were the dean of the College of Liberal Arts and Sciences; the dean of Continuing Education; a divisional chairperson of humanities, natural sciences, or social sciences (a rotating position), and the assistant to the president. Eleven superintendents, who had been previously involved in a variety of programs, joined the four college administrators to make up the fifteen voting members of the steering committee. Since the partnership was on the college campus and college officers had initiated and developed the funded proposal, four additional administrators—the president, the vice-presidents for academic and external affairs, and the executive director of the partnership—sat ex officio on the committee. Among the eleven superintendents was one who led a large consortium of school districts—the Board of Cooperative Educational Services (BOCES)—that enjoyed significant funding from districts throughout the county and political ties to the State Education Department. By having the superintendent of BOCES on the steering committee, the partnership immediately reached beyond its initial eleven school districts and avoided duplication of efforts.

The steering committee is the critical group in a partnership, and its structure must be carefully considered, particularly if the enterprise is to grow beyond its founding members. The original districts will adopt a proprietary attitude toward the partnership. They will not only want to make policy but will want to reserve spaces for their teachers and students in various programs. This makes sense since they will be paying annual dues. Often, however, the partnership districts will not send a sufficient number of participants to a program to justify its existence, and leaders of the program will need to open it to others. Partnership districts must be given first priority, but there must also be a tight deadline for participation in a program, after which time the registration procedure can be broadened to include others. The partnership districts should also pay less than those that are not part of the collaboration. If neighboring teachers and students are invited to participate in programs, the partnership districts will not lapse into complacency, there will be less parochialism, and there will be opportunities for growth.

There is a delicate balance between districts represented on the steering committee and those in the partnership that do not set policy. Superintendents from newly admitted districts will soon come to resent the fact that they are in a subordinate position to the steering committee. If the partnership grows

rapidly, this can become a serious problem. It was in our case.
We solved it by limiting the growth of the partnership to the
forty-six school districts of Westchester County, although educators outside the county were welcome to join after the partnership districts had satisfied their needs. We admitted five new
districts within Westchester County each year and established
rotating memberships on the steering committee, reserving five
permanent spaces for the founding members. With twenty-six
districts in the partnership, we have decided not to extend formal membership beyond Westchester County. A partnership
needs a clear definition.

The constitution of the steering committee is more than
a matter of governance. The issue really is whether the partnership will remain provincial and satisfy only the needs of
local school districts or whether it will embrace a wider audience. There is a final advantage to having a reasonably large
group of school districts. Some superintendents, because of
their own district pressures, are initially passive, joining the
partnership but waiting to see if it will become a permanent
reality. Others may have competing loyalties with local educational organizations, but do not want to be excluded from
a collaboration that might benefit their districts—they join but
do not participate actively. Still others are intensely involved
for a year or two, then withdraw for district or personal reasons. Our steering committee insisted that if a superintendent
missed more than two meetings consecutively out of the four
scheduled each year, he or she had to withdraw from the partnership. The superintendents were their own strictest guard-
ians in this regard, and we had few problems with attendance
or the contribution of district dues. We did have certain superintendents who did not play leadership roles, but these too
were few in number. Apart from the professional pressure of
their peers within a region, superintendents are monitored by
teachers who appreciate the value of academic programs un-
available in their own districts, as well as by board members
and parents who insist on taking advantage of every educational opportunity.

Executive Directors

Of all the figures who must fashion a successful partnership, no one is as crucial as the executive director. The case must be put baldly. A partnership is scarcely possible without a full-time director who is in total control of all administrative details; certainly, this is true of the successful educational collaborations described in Chapter One. If one is serious about institutionalizing the partnership, this first condition is essential, because the authority and responsibility for all activities belong to the director, and they cannot be seriously exercised unless the person is at work Monday through Friday, 9:00 A.M. to 5:00 P.M.—or, more honestly, 8:00 A.M. to 6:00 P.M. and into the evening hours and weekends. A partnership requires a director who does not measure his or her career by the minutes of a clock. The executive director should report directly to the dean, attend the dean's cabinet meetings, and enjoy the same status as department chairpersons and assistant deans.

The role is anomalous and presents numerous difficulties. The executive director is caught between the cultures of the college and the schools; he or she must respond to the superintendents but is also accountable to the dean and the college, unless and until the partnership becomes fiscally autonomous. The director has no tenure or home in an academic discipline and therefore needs to be respectful of independent faculty. By the same token, he or she is not formally affiliated with the superintendents and must handle that delicate relationship carefully. The role is precarious in that the director is forever appealing to college faculty and school administrators for support. He or she is operationally in control of the partnership but is not the true leader of its key participants. The director needs the support of the dean to exercise his or her responsibility effectively and to establish, with each successful project, his or her own authority and independence. Once funding begins to flow into each project, the executive director has of course the greatest power there is—the power of the purse.

The director will be successful because of all those obvious traits one needs in any new administrator: sensitivity to people at all levels of responsibility, the ability to plan effectively as he or she shapes an academic vision and matches expectations to reality, and a self-starting style. The director must also possess intelligence, self-control, and maturity, along with an enormous degree of energy. He or she must have exceptional writing and editing skills for all the proposals that will be drafted, and must possess the appropriate practical experience, especially in the schools. But the director will be short-circuited at every step without the dean's support. In order for the director to work harmoniously with faculty whose academic credentials may be more impressive than his or hers or to engage superintendents whose administrative status is clearly greater or corporate representatives who have independent credentials or even schoolteachers whose salaries are higher—the director needs the academic authority of the dean to assert his or her own authority and to function effectively. As the partnership prospers, the dean's role will diminish.

It is somewhat difficult to specify the appropriate experience required for an executive director. One prefers someone who has taught in the classroom—of the local schools participating in the partnership, if possible. Virtually every project turns upon the teacher, and a director who has been in the line of action carries a credibility that can be helpful. One wants someone with a doctorate, preferably in education, for the authority that degree carries with all participants in the partnership. One needs, more than any other quality, maturity. That characteristic is found most readily in a superintendent, principal, schoolteacher, dean, or faculty member of a school of education who has run the course of his or her career, has approached retirement by his or her midfifties, and sees a second profession with the unlimited possibilities of a partnership. One needs an individual who cares deeply about education and reads the literature, and who is pragmatic and entrepreneurial. Such a person can start work in high gear and capture the respect of the various participants immediately.

Our own record may be of interest. We attracted many candidates, mostly women, and they were often people with the maturity required. The contrast between the two finalists was revelatory. One had impeccable traditional academic credentials but lived outside the area, while the other was a Westchester resident and former teacher in the county who had worked with the superintendents and knew the politics of New York State. The Westchester finalist, Resa Fremed, became our executive director and hit the ground running. With her knowledge of the schools and the State Education Department, she had the pragmatic skills that helped her to know immediately whether a project would work or not, and she could formulate proposals faster than some administrators can write memos. In short, she had all the characteristics essential for an executive director, in addition to being a cyclone of energy. By April 1, 1984, she was appointed; by June 1, she was reporting to work; and by June 13, she had visited each of the superintendents to discover his or her private agenda and secret desires for the partnership. By July 1, she was supervising a proposal for a Math/Science and Computer Training Center, in response to a request for a funded proposal from the State Education Department that brought to meetings (as the state regulations dictated) teachers from each of the eleven school districts; by September 1 the proposal was funded; and in the new academic year, she was meeting the college faculty to measure their strengths and attitudes. Much of this accelerated activity was due to the director's inherent qualities, of course, but they were given immediate focus through her familiarity with the school districts in the partnership.

The executive director's enthusiasm was infectious and had its effect on me, as the dean who related to her most closely. I found myself inevitably drawn into the activities that she had initiated, even though I had initially wanted to draw a clear boundary between my responsibilities to the partnership and my other duties. In fact, I became fascinated by its unfolding possibilities and the almost frightening rapidity of its growth. Three years after our first director was chosen, she resigned to take another position. Her replacement was chosen from many more qualified candidates than had applied when the partnership was first established. He was a recently retired associate dean of education at Queens College, Sidney Trubowitz, who

had successfully led a partnership between a middle school and
Queens College and was prepared to begin a second career and
to help develop the second phase of our partnership.

Project Directors

Each project should be led by a superintendent on the
steering committee, but anyone who knows how a superintendent (or a dean) functions knows that he or she will not do the
work directly and will need a project director as his or her operational leader.

Because superintendents must be actively involved in the
practical administration of each project, we reinforced the structure of the steering committee. We also recognized that superintendents are both extremely busy and always conscious of a
primary responsibility to their districts. Working with them,
the dean, and the executive director of the partnership is the
project director—the academic leader of the program, the person who must create the academic alliance between the schools
and the college, the individual whom everyone else depends upon
for the success of the collaboration.

The project director must be carefully chosen. Our own
method was inductive. As each project organized itself and a
planning committee was formed, a leader naturally emerged.
In the case of mathematics and science, it was a professor of
chemistry at the college; in esthetic education, a retired teacher
in a local school district; in motivation, an elementary school
principal; in economics, a professor of economics at the college.
There is no question that physical and academic control of the
program is far easier if the project director is a college faculty
member, but this is not essential as long as offices are provided
on campus near those of the executive director.

Once appointed, the project director must be compen-
sated—in our case the director was paid $5,000 for the first year
of part-time work, with the clear stipulation that continuation
of the program and compensation depended upon further grants.
Of course, the development of proposals, as I will elaborate in
Chapter Three, is rendered easier than in most cases. One has

the immediate resources of the school districts in terms of their annual dues, the in-service credit that their teachers can earn, and the registration fees they must pay. The schools also provide an initial financial commitment that is extremely compelling when partnership leaders approach foundations and corporations for further support. The operational figure who maintains the integrity and academic excellence as well as the financial development of each activity is the project director; all other leaders are there simply to make his or her work more effective.

Two other points need to be stressed. The project director is primarily the academic leader of the program. Through him or her the workshops, seminars, teaching institutes, and research activities find their curricular focus. In the final analysis, all other leaders of the partnership will depend on this person. The importance of the project director can be illustrated by reference to the director of our programs in mathematics and science. As a professor of chemistry, Carlo Parravano had all the credentials essential for leadership of our projected Center in Mathematics and Science Education. He was, of course, directly connected to the Natural Science Division, and he related all fund-raising activities to the long-range benefit of both that division and the partnership. In addition, by exercising quality control in project after project and by building slowly and sensitively, he gained the support of his colleagues for precollegiate science education. In his classic study of high schools written more than twenty years ago, Conant (1963) recommended the establishment of professors in academic disciplines who would function in the manner of clinical professors in medical and business schools. The director of our Center for Mathematics and Science Education is very close to the realization of that recommendation.

If the project director is in control of all academic matters of the programs he or she supervises, most of the administrative details need to be initially centralized in the offices of the executive director. This may seem a small matter, but if the project director, who after all works only part time, is burdened by administrative and financial details, he or she will soon become frustrated. There is also the danger of losing control of the partnership if fiscal authority is too fragmented. As the project matures, it may be possible to have administrative as well as academic matters decentralized—this is what happened in our math/science programs, once the part-time director occupied a full-time position—but one should resist this direction at the outset. It is also important to keep fiscal control centralized in the partnership offices.

The second point has to do with the need for an associate project director who will implement the program in the schools. If a college faculty member is the project director and therefore the academic leader, he or she will not know the needs of the schools and should have the assistance of a teacher or school administrator. Obviously this structure is ideal and can occur only when the program acquires sufficient financial support, but it suggests the goal that one must continually have in mind as the concept of partnership is woven into every aspect of the collaboration.

3

Key Contributors
to Partnership Success

Although the dean, superintendents, executives, and project directors form the core group of any partnership, other figures soon become essential participants: college faculty and schoolteachers, the community, parents, donors, evaluators, proposal writers, retired executives, and governmental agencies.

College Faculty and Schoolteachers

Teachers form the future of any partnership. It would seem simple to define the role of college faculty and secondary teachers in a partnership until we remember that these two groups have quite different perspectives and career goals. As the president of the College Board has observed:

> The fundamental structural fact about faculty collaboration in the United States is that teachers in the various disciplines are actually divided precisely at the point of the school-college transition. They identify with separate professional organizations—for example, the National Council of Teachers of English on the secondary side and the Modern Language Association on the higher education side. And in doing so, they establish their professional identities in a way that draws an inevitable distinc-

tion between them and their disciplinary counterparts on the other side of the school-college transi-
tion. This is not to say that professional organizations, such as the National Council of Teachers of
Mathematics and the Mathematical Association of
America, do not launch joint projects, but it is to
say that when earlier in this century separate organizations were established in each discipline, one for
essentially higher education faculty and one for secondary school teachers, a great division was opened
in American intellectual life [Stewart, 1987, p. 37].

The college faculty is split between loyalty to their college, where teaching and service are central, and their discipline,
where professional prestige offers the possibility for growth and
career mobility. In contrast, teachers are locked into a school,
and their status depends on their performance in the classroom
unless they leave—as too many of the best teachers do—for administration. College faculty enjoy sabbaticals and leaves of
absence that allow time for research. Although some teachers
do take study leaves, they have little time to read or do research
in their disciplines. Faculty have the academic and financial opportunity for free-lance work in their fields—writing books and
essays, developing scholarly projects, consulting with industry
and business, serving on state and national committees—whereas
teachers too often must find evening, weekend, and summer
work outside the educational field simply to make their total
salary respectable. Faculty control the curriculum and often the
very direction of their college; teachers are bound by bureaucratic rules and regulations. Faculty almost always associate with
colleagues in the same discipline, whereas teachers work in
densely populated settings but are frequently lonely. There are
two different cultures, and their differences must be recognized
if they are to be reconciled.
    A partnership can bridge these cultures, but the burden
rests primarily with the college and especially with the administration of the college. We in liberal arts colleges bear the responsibility of having relegated precollege considerations to programs

in teacher preparation, even as our faculty provide the education for future schoolteachers in their disciplines. We have served on various commissions, have read the reports of declining achievement, and have deplored the poor training students receive in schools. Small wonder that the teachers confront us bearing armor. They feel gratuitous guilt, they feel inferior to college faculty, and they keep the doors of their classrooms shut as tightly as possible. Sarason, as quoted in Trubowitz (1984), makes a cogent distinction between the two cultures:

> In contrast to people in the school culture, faculty in the college or university culture have a far better opinion of themselves. Our centers of higher education have grown in size, support, and status since World War II. In the scores of studies done on the degree of respect and status accorded the different professions, university professors have always been near or at the top and school personnel near or at the bottom of the scale. That difference has not gone unnoticed by professors or school personnel. Unfortunately, professors tend to take this difference (and themselves) very seriously. When they work with school personnel, they tend to expect and to structure relationships in terms of superior-inferior, teacher-student roles. There is something self-defeatingly seductive in the role of "expert," not only for the ambivalence it engenders in the nonexpert (better yet, inexpert) but [for] the insensitivity it can produce in people and their settings. Generally speaking, college faculty truly want to be helpful, just as school personnel want to be effective. The problem is that the value judgments inherent in the distinction between "higher" and "lower" education—one is better, or more important, or more socially worthy than the other—are mirrored in the way relationships between people in the two cultures are perceived and structured when they interact [p. 20].

There can be no greater threat to the success of a college-school partnership than a patronizing posture on the part of the college community toward teachers. Obviously, no dean or leader of a partnership can legislate attitudes, but mutual respect can be encouraged by superintendents on the steering committee, by teachers administering projects and programs, by human interaction in all activities, and most significantly by the college administration. There should not be even the hint of *noblesse oblige*. (Those of us in colleges and universities should be chastened by the fact that some of the recent reports analyzing the state of higher education have been sharply critical.)

The most important distinction between faculty and teachers lies in their working conditions, that is, in the cultures in which they exist. My experience in a partnership has made me far less certain that college teaching is a profession and teaching a job; too many teachers responded hungrily to the professionalism our partnership promised, too many took leadership roles, for me not to conclude that the conditions had to be liberated, not the people. The partnership reminds everyone—the state's department of education, administrators, legislators, faculty and teachers—that the goal of improving the quality of learning for young people makes those teachers engaged in it professionals on a continuum of education.

Even as one makes these traditional distinctions between college *faculty* and school*teachers*—the terms signify the fundamental difference between the two groups—one knows there is a still deeper truth. Because of the unchanging structure of most colleges and because the quality of scholarship is more easily measurable than that of teaching and service, research is rewarded, and faculty search for ways to publish before they perish. Teaching electives is welcome, but working in general education or introductory courses less so, and teaching basic writing and mathematics is anathema. The point, too often, is to teach as little as possible because it is not connected with one's professional advancement—it reduces teaching to a job, to a way of earning a living.

The argument is complicated, I realize, and one would need to speak of graduate school preparation and other aspects of the profession that have created a hierarchy in which research and released time have come to be more desirable than teaching. The root of the problem, however, is a reward system that drives excellent college teachers, who would prefer to remain in the classroom, into producing scholarship that too often is pedestrian and insignificant in comparison with the value of their teaching. The fact is, as Gaudiani and Burnett (1986) have reminded us, few college faculty—fewer than 40 percent in the past two years— have published anything at all; and most faculty members find themselves, like it or not, teaching basic subjects instead of advanced electives. Rather than continuing to view classroom instruction as a punishment, we need to champion, endorse, and reward the teacher, whether he or she is in a college or a school. One of the greatest merits of a partnership is its assertion that teaching is the vital dimension at all levels of education.

College faculty will almost certainly resist a partnership at the outset. They feel that they have earned Ph.D.'s to teach the most sophisticated students that their college or university can attract, and they are professionally not interested in pedagogical matters. Some may participate out of genuine concern; others may contribute because of additional compensation; still others will see the partnership as a recruitment device. But most college faculty will view the partnership as a foreign body invading the traditional organism of the college. It will thus take every effort of the administration—and particularly of the dean, who largely determines the value system of the college—to make the argument that a college-school collaboration is important educationally.

If college faculty are caught in a system that devalues teaching at the expense of scholarship, schoolteachers are treated like children who must respond to all sorts of rules and regulations. It is easy to see why this situation has developed. For example, a "commission on excellence" claims the nation is at risk, invokes standards that the states must impose, and then walks away from the responsibility. Again, statewide regulations are promulgated—New York's standards are particularly rigorous in foreign languages, history, mathematics, and English—and teachers are held responsible for implementing them, even though they have had little to do with initiating these regulations. Teachers are not professionals but civil servants; they do not enjoy genuine autonomy and do not police themselves. They lack intrinsic status not only because their salaries are low but because not enough teachers are sufficiently educated in undergraduate disciplines themselves. Teachers do not shape their own destiny sufficiently. Decision making is taken away from them, and they are burdened by bureaucratic regulations that discourage initiative.

There are many forces that have gathered in recent years to reverse these conditions, the most notable among them being the National Board for Professional Teaching Standards, established in May 1987 as a result of the recommendation of *A Nation Prepared: Teachers for the 21st Century* (1986). Shanker has put the case well. After listing the many virtues of a national board—setting a single national standard while leaving states with the power to license teachers, creating professional autonomy as a consequence of board certification, initiating improvements in teacher training and education, and fostering the public's willingness to provide higher compensation for those who meet these recognized standards—he notes how important it is to convert the job of teaching into the "status of a full profession": "But many people doubt that teaching can ever become a real profession. They think there's an innate difference between teaching and other fields. Of course, teaching is different. No two professions are alike, and teaching will develop in its own way. But if one looks back at what medicine was like early in this century (low prestige, poor pay, rival philosophies of medical practice, low or no standards of entry, and scandalously poor medical education), or law or business administration, we can see that teaching faces no greater hurdle in becoming a full profession than did other occupations" (1987, p. E7).

A collaboration between a college and schools can contribute greatly to the process of making teaching a profession, for it is a magnet for the finest teachers, a meeting ground where they can discuss curriculum and pedagogy in ways that will improve their classroom practice.

The college faculty and the schoolteachers meet in a partnership where improving the teaching of a discipline in the classroom is the solitary aim. The faculty know the discipline, the current status of its scholarship and research, in ways most teachers have not had time to learn; the teachers know what will work in the classroom and take pride in communicating their knowledge. Any partnership that even suggests condescension or patronization on the part of the college professor because he or she possesses a Ph.D. is doomed. Similarly, any hint that the schoolteacher doubts the faculty member's commitment to classroom teaching also threatens the relationship. We will examine this delicate compact more closely when we discuss the implementation of teachers institutes in Chapter Seven.

For now, the point cannot be stressed enough: teachers teaching teachers is the central informing principle of improving education and the heartbeat of any partnership. The National Faculty has provided one of the most dramatic examples of the fundamental importance of teaching. This program has allowed superb college teachers to work with their counterparts in the schools in virtually every state in the country. The most important feature of this partnership program is that the faculty come to the public school site and interact with teachers there, thus expressing respect for the teachers themselves.

Within the SUNY Purchase Westchester School Partnership, I began to see how much teaching can be improved. The first major program developed by our Teachers Center—an organization funded by the State Education Department, with a twenty-one-member policy board of mostly elementary teachers who focused their attention on science education—was led by our professor of chemistry. He helped to train elementary teachers in science instruction and to make them feel more relaxed and comfortable in the laboratory. A core faculty of elementary and high school teachers presented laboratory demonstrations to groups of twenty peers who later translated the demonstrations directly into their own classroom practice; indeed, they left with kits of materials to allow them to do so. In the laboratory demonstration that I observed, two core faculty taught twenty teachers as the college chemistry professor looked on, available if his knowledge was needed. As I watched this simple demonstration, which would have relieved whatever "science anxiety" an elementary teacher might have, I came to realize that there is no substitute for direct contact among college, high school, and elementary school teachers who want to help each other, no replacement for each educator's bringing his or her own special strength to the laboratory and the classroom, and no theoretical, methodological course that can light the fire within teachers so well. What I witnessed was active learning—the equivalent of someone performing on a stage or in a concert hall. The core faculty and the peer teachers were all professionals ready to share their knowledge of chemistry. The college faculty member, who had given a lecture on the scientific method earlier, knew that the magic of learning had occurred that day. As an observer of the process, I perhaps learned even more than the participants. I certainly learned of the need for trust and respect among educators at all levels of learning. It was gratifying to see this happening in the laboratory of a science building on our college campus.

Teachers should serve on advisory committees for each of the programs. Since they will be nominated by their superintendents, support from their school districts is virtually guaranteed, and they in turn will keep the districts actively involved in all the programs. Several examples will illustrate the ways in which these committees can provide a support system for the entire partnership.

Once the director of our Center for Mathematics and Science had established his programs, a process that inevitably brought him into contact with the finest science teachers in the area, he invited forty teachers to serve on an advisory committee. To his surprise, everyone accepted the invitation. The advisory committee was then divided into disciplines—biology, chemistry, mathematics, physics, earth science—and into subcommittees engaged in the development of proposals and other significant activities. The committee has served as a permanent planning, research, and development group that makes any new programmatic developments constantly pertinent to classroom teachers. At the same time, committee members constitute a community of educators throughout the school system.

In foreign languages, a similar approach was designed; in esthetic education, it was primarily English teachers who shaped the program; in economics, social studies teachers developed a curriculum under the guidance of a professor of economics. Each discipline will set up its own advisory committee, which will serve as a counterweight to the steering committee of superintendents. At times, as in the counseling program, it will be advisable to involve not only counselors but those from employment agencies and the personnel offices of businesses; or, as in the leadership program, it will be advantageous to have trainers from corporate programs who can adapt successful business practices to educational administration. But the majority of members on any advisory committee ought to be teachers, counselors, or individuals who play leadership roles within the school.

These advisory committee meetings are fascinating, for the reality of presenting the academic subject dominates every discussion—one enters, as theater people might say, into the subtext of education—and the concept of partnership is reinforced.

Community Friends and Parents

The college/school administrators and teachers can only be as effective as parents will allow them to be. In his recent study, *Education Through Partnership,* Seeley (1985) has written persuasively about the need to have parents involved in an educational partnership. As Theodore Sizer says in his foreword to the book, Seeley grapples with "the apparent contradiction between these two themes espoused by so many of the same people—the theme of centralized authority in education and the theme of the rights of families to have choices among their schools" (p. xvii). Seeley stresses three elements: voice, choice, and loyalty. "The city parents passively acquiesce in the will of a distant government. They may be happy or unhappy about their children's schooling, but, in either case, they have 'no voice in the matter'" (p. 79). Second, parents should have choice. "Choice is a sign of life, of people wanting to take initiative and assume responsibility. Docile acquiescence in whatever the state bureaucracy offers is a sign of the slow death of a people's independence'' (p. 92). Finally, ''loyalty at its strongest not only is integrated with voice and choice but is derived from them'' (p. 101). In some absolute sense, ''partnership requires respect— not just respect for those one agrees with, not just lip service that says school will respect families by doing what the profes- sional staff thinks is best for their children over the objection of their wrongheaded parents—but real respect, which listens to the voices and honors the choices that reflect parents' real values'' (p. 254).

A dramatic example of how a school district can relate effectively to parents and community volunteers occurred in Washington, D.C. ''The first partner of a school district,'' Floretta McKenzie, the former superintendent of the Washing- ton, D.C. school system, has written, ''is its parents and its volunteers. So we are working to revitalize our parent-teacher organizations; even some of our secondary schools now are hav- ing standing room only for PTA meetings. We are also work- ing to improve the quality of the volunteers and the volunteer program. We have moved from 5,000 people volunteering in 1981 in our school district to over 18,000 working in mentor re- lationships, one-to-one tutoring, working in athletic programs— all kinds of ways. We believe that if we can strengthen the in- volvement of the community in the schools, we will reduce the number of students who leave our schools'' (McKenzie, 1987, p. 18).

Without the loyalty of parents, the elaborate structure that I am sketching in this chapter will erode. The best way to elicit support is through solid programs, such as those suggested in Chapters Five through Nine, which will strengthen the educa- tion of their children. But there are also overt ways to gain their support. At the moment when the partnership is solidly an- chored, one can bring together parents and citizens at large into a formally organized group—a ''friends of the partnership.'' Those citizens interested in strengthening education for their community can be included in lectures, conferences, workshops, and seminars designated for them. Their involvement will not only support the partnership as they translate their loyalty into their own participating school systems and whatever political organizations they may belong to, but it could be the first step toward some augmented fund-raising effort. Initially, "friends" can pay annual membership dues of $100 a family—dues that become still another source of partnership revenue. When the partnership has matured sufficiently, support can be sought from individuals and corporations to establish an endowment that will give it greater permanence. This is precisely what is being attempted by Yale University as it seeks to institutionalize the Yale–New Haven Teachers Institute.

The key figures of a partnership are the dean, the superintendents, the executive and project directors, faculty, teachers, community friends, and parents. But others are also essential and need to be defined clearly: the donor, the partnership evaluator and proposal writer, corporate leaders, those who represent other educational enterprises in the region, community leaders, members of the public relations office of the college, and retired executives. A college-school partnership is an educational mosaic of discrete and autonomous units, none of which need it for survival but all of which can profit from its success. These units require sensitive articulation, and their leaders must feel that they own the partnership—it must be theirs, not something given to them. The members of an educational partnership share characteristics common to networks in general. They are "people with something in common, who are not satisfied that their home bases offer them the variety of resources they need to exchange information, learn new things, give and receive help, and fulfill their desires for personal development and for self-expression. Networks are an idea exchange in action settings. Because the settings are detached from the individuals' day-to-day operational base, a wide variety of problems can be addressed more effectively. . . . Neutral ground is the key phrase—the network belongs to everyone and thus to no one" (Cohen and Lorentz, 1977, p. 2).

Donors

We were fortunate in having the American Can (now Primerica) Foundation as our initial donor. The chief executive officer of American Can, William Woodside, had already become a leader in pairing schools and corporations in New York City—American Can had "adopted" Martin Luther King Junior High School. He had also established an American Can Foundation, with Peter Goldberg, a young liberal who had begun his career in the Department of Health, Education, and Welfare during the 1960s as the director and then the vice-president. Goldberg, in turn, attracted educators who found the corporation very sympathetic to social causes.

From the moment that the gift became a possibility, Purchase administrators and the superintendents had concerns about excessive involvement of the foundation director in the operation of the partnership. His visit with us to Albany to help secure the state support he required before he would recommend that American Can make its contribution, his repeated desire to have the partnership replicated even before it was organized at Purchase, and his efforts at greater publicity—these and other expressions of intense interest and eagerness on his part worried those of us at Purchase, but they were of special concern to the superintendents. They were unaccustomed to what the foundation director called a process evaluation. This would engage the evaluator in the partnership as it developed, and would make him entirely accountable to American Can. He would also, however, be available as an adviser to the partnership.

Although these arrangements seemed unusual, they arose from the seriousness with which the donor approached the concept of a college-school partnership. He felt that there was a great need for the private sector to serve as a catalyst for and contributor to educational efforts without the public sector's retreating from its primary responsibility. Even as I worked through preliminary drafts of the original proposal that secured the funding, the donor had retained an adviser—an experienced administrator from the New York City Board of Education, Richard Halverson—who made many valuable suggestions. Rather than feel shadowed or threatened by his comments, I incorporated those that seemed most useful.

The director of the American Can Foundation never intervened in the operation of the partnership, nor did he attempt to shape the direction of its educational programs. But he was insistent that the state university become an active participant, and he withheld support until funding from the university was realized. I remember those early meetings well, especially the director's adamant position: "We want this project to be exportable to other SUNY units. Here we have the possibility for statewide impact in which other SUNY colleges can model programs after ours. But this won't happen if we don't have SUNY and the state involved at the outset, with *their* financial commitment. They must have ownership. We want them to contribute one-third of the funding. Now. At the outset" (Peter Goldberg, personal communication, 1984).

Noble ambitions, I thought, and politically astute, I assumed, but it seemed to me enough to develop something solid locally, to begin modestly. Several years later, I have come to appreciate the tenacity with which the foundation director insisted upon SUNY's partial ownership of the project. I thought that the idea of a statewide and ultimately national model was visionary, although the director probably needed to indulge in this kind of hyperbole to engage support from members of his own board. Now I am convinced, as I will argue in Chapter Ten, that a federal program fostering educational partnerships and challenging business and the educational community ought to be initiated. This program would emulate the National Science Foundation, the National Endowment for the Humanities, and the National Endowment for the Arts. Certainly the director was absolutely right in demanding that SUNY commit itself before American Can would do so. During the fall we visited some key associates of Governor Cuomo who offered their support. The president of SUNY Purchase made the case to SUNY Central, and another faculty line, beyond our normal allocation, was indeed provided. Thus, the private sector "leveraged" the public sector, and this resulted in a faculty line folded into our budget permanently for an executive director of the partnership. Within a year, three more lines were added to our regular budget. It meant institutionalization of the partnership at SUNY Purchase, and a permanence for it that no contribution from a corporation could provide.

Evaluators

A participant who can prove valuable in an educational partnership is a permanent evaluator, someone sympathetic to its growth and development and yet distant enough to be critical of it. The natural tendency is to engage someone to evaluate a project after a fixed period of time. But if finances allow the donor to put a respected educator on an annual retainer, he or she should do so.

In our case, the donor hired the evaluator, and his accountability to American Can kept the relationship between him and partnership leaders clear and objective. A man of vast experience in education, Michael Usdan had worked with James Conant in the sixties on his studies of high schools, moved from professor of education at Northwestern to various other positions, the most notable of which was commissioner of higher education in Connecticut, and now was president of the Institute for Educational Leadership in Washington, D.C. He had also lived in Westchester County for a time and knew the structure of the school districts as well as some of the administrators. The knowledge he brought to us through his national perspective was invaluable, and his belief in the concept of partnership and his desire to make our work successful formed a solid foundation of support for us, especially in the formative stages of our development.

Usdan could also play an important role in engaging the superintendents' support. As we invited seven new school districts to join the partnership in its second year, he pressed the point that they should not become members unless the superintendent would attend meetings regularly and lead particular projects. At an early point, he suggested that the school districts contribute annual membership dues so that when American Can phased out its support, the partnership would be sustained by and institutionalized into the districts.

Needless to say, this contribution from the school districts was the litmus test of their commitment to the partnership and the most sensitive juncture in its development. I had to speak privately to each of the superintendents before the recommendation was introduced publicly, and negotiate what was probably the most critical long-range issue of our partnership. But Usdan was at the meeting when I introduced the idea, and his independent authority, as he supported my recommendation that the districts finance the partnership on an ongoing basis, gave additional weight to my presentation.

It is rare to have so supportive an evaluator as Michael Usdan, but every partnership needs a respected professional who is willing to undertake the task of process evaluation from the beginning. Seasoned educators may well be capable of evaluating a program they have administered, but the perspective of someone not involved with the details of organization is always needed. I do not mean to suggest an evaluation that brings a person or a team to the campus periodically to render a report, but one that genuinely includes the evaluator in the progress of the partnership. All parties want success, in any event, and should develop the evaluation process from that impulse. Needless to say, the chosen evaluator must be disinterested and forceful enough to say the worst to both the donor and the partnership leaders, if warranted.

Proposal Writers

Another important figure who can buttress a partnership is the proposal writer. In fact, the hidden power of a partnership can be most directly located in whoever writes its proposals. This person can be an invaluable resource to the more public figures in the college-school collaboration, not only as a proposal writer but as an ongoing consultant and educational conscience, someone who gives the development of the partnership perspective and proportion.

Our own experience may be instructive. We first took a series of less than satisfactory approaches. One required the executive director and me to spend hours composing each proposal, another involved commissioning a consultant for a special project who proved unsatisfactory and cost us dearly, and a third placed responsibility in a project director who was clearly too busy administering his or her program to pursue funding possibilities.

We finally settled on a retired BOCES executive, Richard Wing, who knew Westchester County and had written proposals extensively during his thirty-year career as an educator. We placed him on a monthly retainer and set up a system in which each project director was in direct communication with him so that he could help guide the development of a proposal. The executive director coordinated the activity and edited drafts, especially in relationship to budgets and administration. I saw a final version and worked with our vice-president for external affairs in submitting the proposal to various agencies. I am convinced that the proposal writer's position outside the formal structure of the partnership gave him an invaluable perspective and made it possible for us to generate proposals more rapidly than would have been possible if we had relied on our own fully employed members. As our relationship matured, I encouraged the writer to serve as a constant critic of all our activities. Over time, he, the executive director, and I formed an administrative and educational core that could anticipate most of the problems presented by our growing partnership.

In every community, there are retired educators and executives who have the time, willingness, and talent to perform the role of proposal writer; they can provide a resource that should not be overlooked.

The Community and Competing Organizations

Beyond the formal participants of the partnership, there is an informal network of college administrators, directors of educational and business associations, community leaders, school board members, and legislators who will inevitably influence its activities, and without whose support, acquiescence, or benign passivity progress can be severely impeded. In addition, unless a partnership is sensitive to the competitive needs of neighboring organizations that also depend on public support, it may not survive.

There is no easy formula for developing a powerful partnership in a community where other educational agencies have thrived; one's success inevitably threatens them. Beyond nourishing the complementary virtues of sensitivity and shrewdness in dealing with competitors, it is necessary to avoid duplication of programs. The critical problem, of course, is asserting the significance of the partnership among those who will be competing for the same state and corporate dollars and who will be appealing to the same school districts for support. By locating the partnership at a college, however, one establishes authority, continuity, and stability immediately. At an early stage in our own development, I attended a series of meetings that had been organized by a competing consortium of college and school representatives, parents, and corporate and community leaders who were eager to create academic programs for the benefit of the schools. A business executive well known in the county was appointed chairperson of the consortium, and a constitution was written with the help of an attorney. But the group never developed a dynamic thrust or became coherent, and the reason was clear: there was no center to it, no college that assumed responsibility for it, no large initial funding that would have allowed it to appoint an executive director. When the meetings were over and their rhetoric a memory, someone needed to bear responsibility for the partnership. The combination of a dean at a college and an executive director reporting to him or her represents that kind of coherent stability.

In our experience, the most serious potential conflict was with the Board of Cooperative Educational Services (BOCES), which reported directly to, and therefore enjoyed the support of, the State Education Department. I mention this relationship because something comparable to it will undoubtedly exist in virtually every community in the country. BOCES covered the entire county and taxed "component" school districts for a variety of services—computerized record keeping, library and computer services, vocational and occupational education, special education for the severely handicapped, bilingual programs, and continuing workshops for teacher training. When districts participated in a given program, they received a subsidy from the state. "Noncomponent" districts could also take advantage of these services on a pay-as-you-go arrangement. The important distinction between BOCES and the partnership, and the one that obviated any unpleasant competitiveness, was that BOCES was a school consortium but had no college or corporation formally associated with it. It did have extraordinary staff and facilities; few private agencies could boast of comparable quality. Our problem was finally more political than educational and required a vigilant effort to establish a healthy relationship between the partnership and BOCES, especially at the beginning, when our collaboration was most vulnerable.

Most of the potential difficulties with BOCES were attenuated by making its superintendent, an extraordinarily open-minded and generous educator, Richard Lerer, a member of our steering committee. At each juncture, we asked ourselves whether BOCES, with its sizable administrative structure, might be a more effective delivery system for a program. We tried to avoid duplication, but the relationship was inevitably competitive; and, as in any competition, the stronger one is, the more respected one becomes. The partnership had the powerful central presence of the college, a status superintendents and their associates enjoyed. The partnership had a special configuration—the college, the schools, the private sector—that was not confined by state regulations but instead allowed for flexibility and rapid implementation of programs. Because of other relationships that the college had established with local companies, the partnership had access to corporations and foundations; because of its connections to the school districts, it was also in contact with the State Education Department; because of the college itself, it reached into SUNY and other agencies of higher education. As we secured significant funding, we became an educational force in the county and finally in the state.

The creation of presence is a never ending public relations activity that initially can be carried on by the college but may ultimately need to be incorporated into the partnership itself. A newsletter to all schools in the community, not only those in the partnership, is mandatory. Periodic breakfasts or meetings with legislators and community leaders should be held for progress reports: most of the funding, especially in today's political climate, will emerge from state sources, and it is essential to have legislative advocates. The key recommendation for all these activities is openness. Academic paranoia is a by-product of any newly developed enterprise, and the political ramifications among groups are finally unique to each community. But the partnership is inevitably so public that any inclination to confidentiality with a steering committee of more than ten superintendents should be avoided. Most of the superintendents and their colleagues belong to competing organizations, in any case, and they naturally seek what is most profitable for their districts. By putting them in charge of particular projects in the partnership, they will become the eyes and ears of the community and remain loyal to the partnership.

The executive director and I held Friday breakfasts in my office with influential figures, with no agenda other than a description of partnership activities. We had an annual cocktail and dinner party to thank all participants, and we remembered to invite community leaders who could be helpful. We published an annual report listing all our accomplishments that was broadly distributed. In time, our mailing list swelled to include the forty-six school districts in Westchester County and more than fifty others in Nassau, Rockland, Putnam, and Orange counties, as well as parts of New York City, the colleges in the New York metropolitan area, and other educational organizations throughout the entire region. Our communications both alerted everyone to what we were doing and advised competitors that, although we intended to be cooperative, we also intended to pursue our goals relentlessly. The balance, as every administrator knows, is delicate, but it can be achieved.

Retired Executives

Retired executives in the community can provide an invaluable source of support for partnership leaders and a further extension into the community. The International Executive Service Corps originally sent retired executives to aid Third World nations in their management practices. The late Frank Pace, who was its president, adapted this concept to various aspects of education, forming a National Executive Service Corps. With funds from the Carnegie Corporation of New York, the National Executive Service Corps sent out questionnaires to retired executives and military leaders and received some 4,300 responses. The results were interesting: "Seventy percent of industry respondents and 79 percent of military respondents reacted favorably to exploring a postretirement teaching position." Roughly one-third showed interest, 38 percent "qualified their interest depending on teacher qualifications and the availability near their school. Only 29 percent had no interest" (Pace, 1987, p. 2). The organization plans to prepare prospective retirees from corporations for certification in the schools. Workshops at the business site, equivalent to education courses, will allow the executives to move directly into the classroom upon their retirement.

The White Plains High School in Westchester County has been working for some time with three executives placed there by the National Executive Service Corps. One, with a science background, is associated with an astronomy teacher; the second, retired from New York Telephone, is involved with computers; and the third, whose background is in organizational development and personnel, serves as a resource teacher to a planning team. Retired executives will soon be working with teachers and staff members in a cable television studio as well as in social studies, English, and business departments. Principals can also use people with organizational skills as consultants for various projects. Furthermore, for elementary school pupils whose teachers may be predominantly women, just seeing and relating to more men in a school context may be a beneficial experience.

Encouraging retired executives to take up teaching as a second career, especially in mathematics and science, offers one interesting solution to the problem of hiring a sufficient number of qualified teachers. Unions appear to be supportive, as long as the plan conforms to their policy of never replacing a teacher with a volunteer. Integrating retired executives into the teaching institutes provides an ideal way of familiarizing them with the latest trends in classroom pedagogy and subject matter. Beyond formal teaching, retired executives can serve many other functions in the partnership itself: writing publication relations documents and editing reports; collecting data and developing questionnaires; assisting with budgetary questions and preparing financial reports; speaking to parents on the relationship between education and business; lobbying state agencies and aiding with fund raising; advising administrators about organization and management; helping superintendents and principals with community relations; coordinating special activities and events such as science or book fairs and radio and television programs; assisting teachers in making audiotapes for class use; editing the school newspaper or magazines; serving as the liaison for work experience programs; and most importantly, working directly with students as tutors in academic and nonacademic subjects. Retired executives can function as supplementary instructors in academic resource centers, conducting small-group activities, lecturing to classes on selected topics, and helping in the library and media center.

The list, clearly, is as long as the activities of the school itself. There will be need for a staff coordinator in the partnership, but two of the executives should be largely responsible for organizing and administering any effort that is mounted—co-chairpersons, so that one can spell the other. Retired executives can exist as a separate group within the partnership, but a logical place for them is in the Center for Leadership Development, with close links to the guidance counselor program (described in Chapters Eight and Nine). All the possible contributions mentioned above should be developed in terms of task forces—specific tasks assigned for a specified period of time. In this way the executives can vary their activity and sustain their interest. Whatever assignments are made to the retired executives must be meaningful. These task-oriented individuals have low tolerance for boredom, make high demands as a result of their own success, and possess great energy. They must know that their work is significant or they will withdraw from the partnership. By integrating them into the Center for Leadership Development and the guidance counselor program, partnership leaders allow them to continue their roles as leaders—in education now rather than in business.

Government

The final participant of any educational partnership must be government. The states have already responded to partnerships

and have often been leaders in the first wave of the reform movement. Chance's study of seven activist states, *The Best of Educations* (1986), indicates that not only have governors and legislators
been the driving force behind educational innovation, but they
have listened closely to educators and used their ideas. They
have generated the force needed to bring about educational
reform: "Linkages between the nation's economic well-being
and academics have found expression at all levels of government, determining the tone, content, and shape of responses
to what has become and seems to have remained a commonly
acknowledged crisis. . . . The reassertion of ownership implied
by the political nature of the present reform movement represents
a direct, if unheralded, challenge of important traditional pre-
sumptions about the educability of students, about the omni-
science of professionals, about a public presence in the locus
of control. More than this, and maybe willy-nilly, the political
response is predicated on the brash assertion that all children
can learn, and all should be educated. This makes the risk worth
taking" (Chance, 1986, p. 1).

Chance's book reviews the process of political change in
California, Colorado, Florida, Illinois, South Carolina, Texas,
and Washington, and concludes that although educational reform has been distinctly political, "educators also played a significant, if sometimes unappreciated, role in many states. In
no case, however, was an individual, such as governor or state
school superintendent, able to accomplish the changes alone.
Political coalitions were necessary in all of the major change
states" (p. 6).

Governors such as Richard Riley of South Carolina,
Lamar Alexander of Tennessee, Thomas Kean of New Jersey,
John Ashcroft of Missouri, and Bill Clinton of Arkansas have
been sensitive to the need for collaborations that include government as a catalyst and have placed education at the head of agendas necessarily crowded with other pressing social needs. At the
1987 National Governors' Conference, Kean challenged the
federal government and directed a range of questions that he
felt ought to be asked of presidential aspirants: "Candidates
should be asked what they would do to improve the education

of the urban and rural poor, how they would link federal education aid to educational quality, how they would connect education
to welfare reform and employment policies. They should be
asked . . . how they would encourage Americans to spend more
on higher education and how they would shore up research"
(Hechinger, 1987b, p. C11).

   In New York, Governor Cuomo has established the School
and Business Alliance, cochaired by Saul Cohen, whose focus
is "a job pledge program that [will] motivate at-risk youngsters
to graduate from high school and, if they [succeed] in acquiring various work-to-transition skills while in school, provide them
with employment opportunities" (Cohen, 1987, p. 64). The goal
has already been enlarged to "help schools better serve all students by connecting learning, motivation, and employment
consciousness. Similar school-business partnerships have been
started in Atlanta, Boston, Miami, Philadelphia, and Seattle,
but New York is the first to launch a statewide, publicly initiated
and funded effort" (p. 64). A governmental initiative, as Cohen
points out, can tap into the vast resources of the state; the lia-
bilities of such an initiative need to be guarded against too—
the danger that "the corporate and labor worlds may not feel
sufficiently invested in the enterprise. . . . Neither government
nor the school system alone can solve the education crisis. But
a network of business, labor, education, and local communities
can. In a true alliance, the burden for the success or failure of
the schools is on all sectors. When partnerships succeed, all of
the owners benefit. When partnerships fail, all of the owners
lose. There is no school-partnership program which has come
close to reaching this stage" (p. 65). The reason, I would argue,
is the absence of leadership, of a cohering force that gives definition to partnership. As large social and economic forces, including government, seek to aid the educational enterprise and
grow more manifest, the need for a leader will become ever
greater. Government itself, as a strong ally, will rightly seek
guidance from its colleges and schools. And within the educational community, leadership should emerge from higher
education.

   A partnership is an educational mosaic that must respect

the autonomy of each participant as it makes the case that only through collective effort will excellence be achieved. The creation of this mutual estate must be the work of a central academic figure at a college and will require a good measure of selflessness on the part of that person. His or her duties will be increased, probably without compensation, and he or she will be sorely tested in trying to persuade the faculty that this effort is crucial to the college. For a partnership is more than an interaction of schools, colleges, businesses, governmental agencies, and the community; more than different groups bringing issues that relate only to themselves; more than a meeting of strangers, who become associates, colleagues, even friends. A partnership is a fusion of concerned citizens who must put aside their private motivation for the moment and focus upon the enhancement of student learning. It is the equivalent of Keats' negative capability: seeing the poem for itself; seeing education for itself.

The schools have teachers who know what will work in the classroom and are primarily concerned with illuminating the subject for their students. But these teachers are also interested in the subject itself and want to function as chemists, physicists, and historians—they want to repossess their disciplines.

College faculty are trained in graduate schools to do scholarship and not to teach, even though they will spend most of their careers teaching. Too often they are rewarded for scholarship and research reluctantly pursued—usually only for promotion and tenure. Many of these faculty members would like to work with teachers in the classroom and should be rewarded for doing so in colleges of liberal arts and sciences.

Business executives and the directors of corporate foundations are eager to support educational projects, sometimes because the children of their employees are in neighboring schools, sometimes because the project will be of direct benefit to their corporation, sometimes as a corporate gesture of public support or community relations. Whatever their motivating principles, they have become more generous than ever before. They have come to see their own future intertwined with that of the schools.

The community has an advisory role that can never be

underrated because it exerts pressure on the other three groups. The community is always advisory, but its advice and counsel, its participation, and its psychological ownership strengthen every project. As a partner, it takes the project into the home for nourishment that is critical. Parents can be the most supportive partners. They know, through their children, how valuable partnership activities are and they will make certain superintendents and teachers participate actively.

Government can furnish enormous resources and help to replicate the partnership throughout the state. It can exert pressure on the university's budget by making school-college partnerships a high priority, it can serve as a catalyst for new programs, and it can provide funds that will leverage support from the private sector. Our own experience with a variety of activities— establishing a new Teachers Center, publishing a demographic study of New York's educational future, issuing a conference report, securing support for different academic programs— confirms my belief that the largest source of financial as well as political support for partnerships will come from the state departments of education and from state government itself.

And through the regard of schoolteachers and administrators, college faculty, corporate friends, community leaders and families, and governmental leaders for one another; through the networking that will inevitably occur between these different groups; through the intellectual coherence that a college can provide, a mutual estate can be created.

4

Developing Financial
and Institutional Support

There is no single funding model that applies to all partnerships, but there are two elements that will contribute to their long-term success. The college or university must be completely supportive of the enterprise, and significant initial funding from an external donor must be secured.

Commitment from the university is critical. Without it, the Bay Area Writing Project at Berkeley, the Yale–New Haven Teachers Institute, and Syracuse University's Project Advance—to cite but three examples—would never have been launched. Similarly, the SUNY Purchase Westchester School Partnership was made possible because the university's president, Sheldon Grebstein, and his entire administration championed it from the outset as the major public service effort of the College of Liberal Arts and Science. Whatever financial support may be found in local corporations, businesses, foundations, and state or federal agencies, one's own institution finally bears the heaviest cost and must anchor the partnership.

The cost to a college is considerable and should not be minimized. It begins with the allocation of space—rooms for the director, secretary, and other staff support—and the location of that space, preferably near the dean's office. It includes sufficient supplies and equipment, for the growth of the partnership depends heavily on the generation of grant proposals. It involves at least a temporary reduction of the indirect overhead cost of each grant proposal—in our case the normal 39.9 percent for salary and wages was lowered to 12.4 percent—so that a firm foundation of support can be established.

The greatest expense, and certainly the one most difficult to measure, will take the form of administrative time. In the initial stages of our own partnership, when the proposals needed to be written and the entire enterprise had to be organized, I devoted at least 50 percent of my total efforts to the college-school collaboration. Other colleagues, who helped in a variety of ways, had to carve out time from their primary administrative obligations until the partnership was fully institutionalized through my office. This work can later be delegated to an associate or assistant dean, but at the outset the dean will have to be deeply involved. The superintendents will not work personally with a partnership unless the dean or provost of the college, representing the president, demonstrates his or her active interest in it; and faculty members of the college need to witness this personal participation before they will really believe that this is a genuine part of the reward structure and can contribute to their own reappointment, tenure, and promotion.

Obtaining Outside Support

Most partnerships begin with a grant from some external agency. The Bay Area Writing Project, for example, secured significant support from the Carnegie Foundation before it drew further funds from the National Endowment for the Humanities and became the National Writing Program. The Yale–New Haven Teachers Institute was initially funded by the National Endowment for the Humanities and then found support from local corporations. The Public Education Fund was underwritten by the Ford Foundation and the Boston Compact by local businesses.

Our own project was made possible by the American Can Company, and its funding origins may be of interest to other colleges located near sizable businesses or major corporations. The original intention of the American Can leaders was very generally stated: American Can would like to be of service to the local schools. Despite the fact that the corporation was located in Greenwich, Connecticut, it was prepared to support a proposal (upwards of $500,000 for five years) that would bring a college of the State University of New York into association with the Westchester schools to improve the quality of education for youngsters. As the eleven founding superintendents and I worked together on the proposal, we never experienced any corporate control over the educational goals set forth, the budgetary allocation for programs, or the programs themselves. There was, however, one major point of resistance that was irritating at first but ultimately proved to be of great importance to the success of the partnership. The donor insisted that one-third of the funding come from the state university so that it would have ownership of the project and seek to replicate the concept throughout its sixty-four campuses. As it turned out, the university, stimulated by the original American Can gift, provided more support than we had expected—an original line for the executive director and, in the following year, three additional lines for a science director, an assistant director, and another staff position—at a time when our campus enrollments were stable and no additional funding was forthcoming for any other sector of the campus. The special configuration of the college, the schools, and corporation stimulated funding because it reached beyond the campus and suggested growth and a larger vision.

But these stipulations by American Can are finally details. The essential point is that without the five-year commitment of the corporation, which was subject to annual review by its own process evaluator, the project would never have been launched or continued. It stimulated further funding in both the public and private sectors, especially among other corporations in the county. Once a corporation has successfully initiated a program, however, it must inevitably withdraw and then go on to another frontier. Woodside has put the case well: "But we must carefully define roles and responsibilities. Business is not government. Public-private partnerships should not mean private-sector substitution for public-sector responsibility. Business can and should support government by contributing financial leverage, but not by assuming the financial responsibilities of government nor the educational responsibilities of educators. When we can craft an appropriate role for business participation, however, we should pursue it with dedication and with vigor'' (1984, p. 1).

This is precisely what American Can did in our case. Initially we thought that we would receive $500,000 over a five-year period, but the grant actually provided $110,000 for start-up expenses in the first two years, $70,000 for the third year, and $30,000 each for the fourth and fifth years. This brought the total to $240,000. We obviously could have spent the remaining $260,000 and expanded further and faster, but the squeeze on us worked well and caused us to push harder to secure other funds. The total of $240,000 was enough to help create the partnership—that and the addition of the four permanent lines from the state university. Every college, every group of school districts, every community should be equally fortunate.

Fund Raising

The funding formula for proposals ought to be tripartite. No project should be initiated unless it has the support of several school districts. This can be guaranteed by the presence of one superintendent as leader of each project and of two others who serve on the project committee with him or her. These superintendents carry not only the promise of funding but the knowledge of what will work in their districts. Support from the schools will be matched by the college or university in the form of supplies, equipment, space, personnel, reduced overhead on grants, and fiscal contributions. With the schools and college solidly behind each effort, a proposal to a state or federal agency, corporation, or foundation stands a great chance for success. This tripartite formula also opens up possibilities that are closed to a single school district or college.

Corporations prefer to support a consortium of school districts and a college rather than a single district or institution. As Goldberg notes, the Westchester County school system is fragmented and heterogeneous.

> There are forty-six separate and autonomous school districts. They vary in nature by a considerable degree. There are urban school systems, suburban

school systems, rural school systems. There are
school systems which serve the very affluent; there
are school systems in the county which provide
educational opportunities for lower-income people.
There are large school systems and there are small
school systems. It is a most heterogeneous county.
It is impossible for the business community to relate
to all forty-six school districts at the same time in
any kind of systematic way on a one-by-one basis.
Similarly, it is impossible for those forty-six separate
school districts to each develop a meaningful relationship with all the area businesses in Westchester
county. And as you well know, there are a number
of large corporations that are headquartered in
Westchester County that ought to be responsible
to and helpful to these school systems. . . . The
partnership has thus offered a single, effective mechanism by which the business community can address the needs of multiple school districts. And I
think that in many respects, from the business perspective, that coalition concept has been a significant ingredient in the development and maturation
of this partnership. The partnership is one locus
point by which the corporate community can work
with all these different school districts. I think that
the idea of housing the partnership through a local
college—having a local university be the umbrella
mechanism—is an added benefit to this whole partnership concept [Goldberg, 1987, p. 70].

As the partnership grows and a fund-raising strategy
develops, the need for centralized control of all proposals will
become apparent. The project directors who work with the superintendents should be held responsible for generating proposals, but their ideas can be developed in collaboration with a proposal writer and must be shared with the executive director and
the dean, who will need to join them when the proposals are
presented for funding. In any college-school partnership with

multiple project directors and various sources of revenue, tight control over the process of fund raising is mandatory. In our case, we processed all our monies through the SUNY Research Foundation, an agency whose counterpart can be found in every college or university. This meant paying a specially arranged and remarkably low indirect overhead cost of 12.4 percent. It also meant abiding by certain bureaucratic constraints, which were sometimes frustrating, but it gave us total control over all revenues and created an audit trail. As soon as funding allowed, we hired a budget officer who had dealt directly with the Research Foundation. Although the directors are now given increased autonomy as their projects mature, this officer serves as the overseer of all budgetary matters for the partnership.

Financial Management

A critical turning point in the development and administration of any partnership will be the moment when the school districts are asked to contribute regularly to its long-range support. As Wilbur has recently observed, many partnerships "do not have hard line budgets, but rather are funded from year to year or are dependent on funding from an agency whose priorities tend to change with the wind" (1987, p. 38). The degree of financial support from the school districts determines whether the enterprise will be transitory or institutionalized.

In our experience, that test came in the middle of the second year—after all the districts had committed themselves to the partnership, after the programs had been set in place and many teachers had participated, after the structure of the collaboration was clear, and after American Can, the State University of New York, a number of other corporations (IBM, Texaco, Pepsico), and the State Education Department had provided support for individual projects. We devised a formula based on the number of students in each district. For larger and, in one case, financially constrained school systems, we placed a cap on the dues structure. Our original funding formula and the annual dues we taxed each district appear in Resource B.

There is no magic formula; in fact, the formula itself

hardly matters. The critical need is to persuade the districts that they must take ownership of the partnership, and the only way that can happen is through their direct financial support of it. Once the districts see the benefit of the partnership to their own teachers and students, the dues will be paid with equanimity and rarely be questioned.

Beyond these annual dues, the districts paid $150—raised to $160 two years later—for each teacher registering in one of our institutes, furnished seed money for special projects that their superintendents initiated, and provided staff development funds for teachers attending seminars, workshops, and conferences. These fees create no problem for the districts or their teachers— some of whom paid themselves—but they can be called into question when the National Science Foundation or the National Endowment for the Humanities or a union-based Teachers Center offers stipends for teachers to attend the same or similar institutes. There is no simple way to reconcile such a disparity, but it is critical to have the teachers or their districts pay a nominal fee, just as it is critical to keep the costs of the institutes as low as possible. Stipends supported by external agencies are ephemeral; institutes temporarily funded in this way may be attractive one summer or one year, but then significant funds must be secured to sustain them. If one is truly serious about institutionalizing a partnership, the costs must be dispersed among the participating school districts and the college, and they need to be kept to a minimum.

This incremental pattern of persuading the different constituencies in a partnership to intensify their commitment would seem fairly typical. The partnership needs the stimulus of an external donor; it must have the ongoing support of the college and university; it should begin the process of generating funds from foundations, corporations, state and federal agencies; and it should secure, fairly early in its development, the ongoing commitment of the school districts. Confidence in this new structure is created by balancing each constituency against the other— by having each strengthen the other. In this way the partnership becomes institutionalized.

Institutionalization

More needs to be said specifically about institutionalizing an educational partnership. It should be located at a college or university willing to take full and final responsibility for its future. A program such as advanced placement may exist independently, but a collaboration or consortium that relates to the schools, corporations, and community of a specific area needs a permanent home in an educational institution. School districts may support the partnership for a time and then, because of difficulties with finances or the resistant attitude of a new superintendent, withdraw. The college has the appropriate resources to house a partnership: an office for external affairs prepared to facilitate fund raising and publicity; faculty members who, unlike teachers in the schools, are disposed to research and scholarship and have the time to prepare proposals and keep alert to developments in academic disciplines; and a research foundation for processing all grant proposals. Finally, the college both represents neutral ground and confers status and prestige on the partnership.

Superintendents are inevitably rivals in a way that does not relate to college administrators; they need to satisfy their school board members who are conscious of what is occurring in neighboring, competing districts. The superintendents and many of their associates have higher degrees and enjoy a formal relationship to a college or university, and they may eventually teach in some of its programs. Indeed, many work as adjuncts in colleges as a matter of course. In our experience, superintendents, other school administrators, teachers, and especially students enjoyed coming to the college for meetings, workshops, seminars, and conferences. The relationship between the schools and college is more than convenient—it is mutually beneficial and professionally nourishing in the deepest sense.

If the college is the administrative home of the partnership, the dean's office should be its hearth. Except in institutions where there are formal programs in education, every effort should be made to locate the partnership in liberal arts and

science. A college-school collaboration should not be an append-
age to traditional academic disciplines; it should be the foundation for higher learning. By integrating it administratively
in the college and by developing associations among superintendents and teachers, college administrators and faculty, all parties
to the partnership create a community of learning that reinforces
the concept of one educational process. We return, finally, to
what Henry Morrison Clinton wrote, in telling words, more
than sixty years ago: "As a people, we do not think in terms
of education; we think in terms of schools. We have no educational system; we have an elementary school, a high school, and
a college" (1923, p. 73). Without violating the integrity and
autonomy of each level of learning, a college-school partnership located at a college campus begins to create an educational
system.

The clearest evidence of whether an educational system
has been created will be found in the relationship of academic
programming to the administration. There has developed a
hierarchy in education that implies a growing order of status,
from elementary to graduate school and from teacher to administrator. We administrators are often guilty of forgetting that
we serve faculty and students, who are engaged in the primary
act of learning, and we have built structures—offices for fund
raising, governmental affairs, and community relations—that
sometimes reinforce the administrative bias of this academic
hierarchy. In the school districts one witnesses a similar division
of authority that seems, at least in the eyes of this observer, even
more hierarchical—superintendents have an authority that is
awesome in comparison to that of an academic dean. Here, too,
we must reassert the central truism, too often blurred, that the
center of the educational enterprise is academic, not administrative.

At the same time, the administrative structure of educational partnerships is obviously fundamental to efficiency. The
critics of A Nation Prepared (1986) seem justified in suggesting
that a committee of teachers cannot replace a principal in running a school; so too a partnership will flounder without a strong

leader. It is not accidental that every vital partnership has a key figure as its advocate.

If Emerson was right in saying that an institution is the long shadow of a single leader, a partnership is still another example; its leadership devolves on a dean and an executive director. But it also depends on the harmonious configuration of divergent individuals, each of whom is a leader in his own institution and all of whom come together to form a new design and to shape a new purpose. The following five chapters are devoted to the programs that we developed for students, teachers, counselors, and leaders—the central constituencies of our collaboration—and suggest some major approaches that can be adapted by any educational partnership. They are not definitive, only suggestive of the potentialities of partnership. I have assumed that the reader agrees that all these programs are needed: that gifted students are not fully served, especially in small school districts, and that at-risk students present one of the most serious problems for all schools but particularly for those in cities; that teachers of mathematics and science, of economics, foreign languages, and many other disciplines are in need of training and retraining; that a program in leadership can be beneficial to school and college administrators, teachers, students, and governmental and community representatives. I have avoided reiterating the need for these programs and gone directly to questions of implementation and practice, offering one large pragmatic response, in the form of an educational partnership, to the central problem of improving the quality of learning in American schools.

5

Programs to Increase Students'
and Teachers' Motivation

When the SUNY Purchase Westchester School Partnership was formally established in April 1984, the chief executive officer of the American Can Company described the goals of the collaboration with apt precision. He recognized that a partnership of eleven school districts would allow his corporation to support education throughout an entire community rather than show preference to a single district: "The SUNY Purchase–Westchester School Partnership Program is a partnership of uncommon characteristics. It is a partnership between a state government and a private corporation; a partnership between a state university and municipal school districts; and it is a partnership among the eleven heterogeneous participating school districts themselves. Most important, this is a partnership of relationships through which projects will continuously be explored and developed in a systematic way" (Woodside, 1984, p. 2).

The educators in this partnership pledged that they would respond pragmatically to the numerous reports that had criticized American education, and especially to *A Nation at Risk* (National Commission, 1983), with its vision of a rising tide of mediocrity in the land. They and their faculties would deal organically and directly with the needs of the schools and invite the corporate and governmental sectors, as well as the community to share the partnership with them.

The programs presented in the following four chapters have a brief but interesting history and form the evolution of

this partnership. When our steering committee of eleven superintendents and four Purchase administrators first defined the
goals of our collaboration, we asked ourselves a simple question:
What are the critical issues of American education? There was
no formal process by which we arrived at these goals; nor did
the college administrators, who had not engaged themselves professionally with the schools, contribute to the formulation of
them. Eleven superintendents drew upon their collective experiences and on all that they had read and offered the following
answers:

- *The academic expectations of colleges:* What academic expectations do colleges and universities have of their own students?
  What are the common problems of high schools and colleges?
- *Strengthening the foundations of the educational experience:* How can
  the foundations of the educational experience, especially in
  the elementary schools, be strengthened? How can sequential study in academic skills and content be clarified and
  reinforced?
- *Establishment of colloquia for school board members and others responsible for educational policy:* How can the major ideological and
  pragmatic issues that affect the schools be considered most
  effectively by school board members and administrators?
- *Improving instructional effectiveness:* How can we make better
  use of the 180 days currently allocated to the school year?
- *Motivating the unmotivated student:* How can we motivate the
  unmotivated and the underachieving students—not only the
  highly gifted but the average too?

It was as good a list as any, although we knew that these
were broad concerns that needed to be reshaped and focused
in terms of specific projects. In other words, they needed to be
converted into hard reality. That conversion process was in
essence the creation of the real partnership, for it brought everyone together in the formulation of several major programs: an
institute for *motivating* students and teachers; projects for gifted
and talented *students* as well as for those at risk; *teacher-training*
institutes in the disciplines; fellowships for *guidance counselors* that

would relate the world of learning to the world of work; and a *leadership* development center that would help to create the partnership we were initiating.

Motivation of Students and Teachers

A central theme of any partnership must be the motivation of both students and teachers in their common objective of improving learning. An "institute for motivation" or its equivalent can draw upon the most important motivational theory, indicate how it can be put into practice, and have a considerable effect on the many students and teachers who participate in the partnership.

A significant body of literature has developed in the field of motivation. Madeline Hunter, Raymond Wlodkowski, Kenneth Eble, Stanford Ericksen, Patricia Cross, and Arthur Chickering are some of the most sensible commentators on how teachers can improve their effectiveness. In our own instance, we turned to the principles of Hunter (1985a, 1985b) and Wlodkowski (1985), which are particularly compelling and useful as one confronts the reality of the classroom. Their principles undergird the implementation of the programs for students, teachers, and counselors that we will subsequently discuss.

In a series of publications that describe how theory can be translated into practice, Hunter has maintained that "techniques that affect students' motivation are teachable. Properly coached, teachers can learn and practice them. Resulting achievement reduces teachers' feelings of impotence and students' dark suspicions that trying is futile" (1984, p. 4). Hunter stresses that the material learned in the classroom must be related to the life concerns of students and everything taught (except perhaps advanced math and science) should have a parallel in the students' experience, even if that experience is narrow and impoverished. In *Prescription for Improved Instruction and Mastery Teaching,* she spells out specific techniques: "raising or lowering a student's level of concern about the learning; deliberately adjusting feeling tone to pleasant, unpleasant, or neutral; introducing novelty or vividness; giving immediate and specific feedback; and, most important, enabling the student to realize success as a result of effort'' (1984, p. 4).

Wlodkowski concentrates on the learning situation within the classroom. Each situation can be divided according to a "time continuum." In the beginning phase, the student enters and starts the learning process, establishing certain attitudes toward the general learning environment, the teacher, subject matter, and him- or herself; the student has certain needs that must be satisfied at the time of learning. The middle phase encompasses stimulation processes that affect the student during the learning experience and depend heavily on the affective or emotional experience of the student while learning. The final phase stresses competence—"the competence value for the student that is a result of the learning behavior" (1985, p. 1) and "the reinforcement value attached to the learning experience for the student" (p. 19). Once these factors are understood, the teacher can "facilitate student motivation, prevent motivation problems, and . . . diagnose motivational potential in learning situations" (p. 21). Wlodkowski's motivational model is based on a time continuum that can be seen in microcosm in the fifty-minute classroom and, extending outwards, in the entire semester's work, the student's college career—the student's life.

Establishing an Institute for Motivation

Hunter and Wlodkowski are two of the finest advocates of motivational theory, and their ideas are being used in many school districts to great effect. Our own institute translated their ideas as well as those of other theorists into practice. The training model lasts for two years and seeks "to identify, practice, and replicate teacher-based instructional strategies for increasing student willingness to learn" (Russell and Colletti, 1986, p. 2). In the first year, ten teachers in grades 4 and 5 and five principles interact with experts in motivational theory and practice (Wlodkowski joined our institute for a demonstration of his ideas) in an intensive eight-day training program. The fifteen educators come in groups of three, each from a school district so that a building-level team is formed that ultimately introduces

the motivational practice into the schools. They continue the
training process through the first school year in their five school
districts. During that first year, each building-level team provides a coaching experience for other teachers in their own
schools on an ongoing basis, meeting biweekly and reporting
on successful methods, identifying useful materials, and validat-
ing motivational strategies. The work results in a teacher's
guidebook on motivation and the development of a core faculty
that is prepared to act as coteachers in the campus school and
in the Institute on Motivation.

In the summer of the second year, a four-week campus
school for elementary grade students is established. Ten to twelve
students from grades 4 and/or 5, in each of the school districts,
are carefully selected to provide heterogeneous grouping and
to participate in the school program; thus the campus school
serves as a laboratory for the Institute on Motivation and allows
administrators and teachers to apply principles of motivation
in a classroom setting. The institute, which is centered around
a school program, is "designed to serve approximately sixty
elementary pupils, ten teachers, and five principals. The intent
of the school component [is] to allow core faculty the opportunity to further develop motivational techniques in a realistic environment: the classroom. Project staff [are] grouped into three
member teams consisting of two teachers and one principal and
[are] responsible for approximately ten to twelve students per
teaching team" (Russell and Colletti, 1986, p. 8).

Five districts have participated in the Institute on Motivation, each making a two-year commitment to the project at the
level of $2,500. The instructional approach to the school reflects
the "effective schools" research, which claims "that schools can
make a large difference in learning and that the administrator
is a key element in school effectiveness" (Lane and Walberg,
1987, p. 2). This research incorporates the following elements:
"team teaching, experiential learning, ongoing adaptive planning,
and master teaching. Class lessons [are] scripted by team members in an attempt to identify effective motivational strategies.
Curriculum content [emphasizes] language arts and mathematical problem solving as vehicles to apply motivational techniques.

Pupils [engage] in individual, small-group, and large-group learning activities'' (Mix, 1985, p. 1).

The staff development model that incorporates the Summer Training Institute, bimonthly debriefing meetings, and the campus school component are essential elements of our program, which is called Motivational Opportunities to Reach Excellence (Project MORE). We have become convinced that the original hypothesis that inspired the institute has proven true: teachers can become more effective by incorporating motivational processes into their teaching, and students in the campus school, who have perceived the ''learning environment to be satisfying, cohesive, and competitive'' (Russell and Colletti, 1986, p. 8) bring these attitudes to their work during the academic year. A program of this kind has enormous value in sensitizing all educators, and especially the indifferent teacher, to the need for motivation, and it marries theory and practice within the classroom.

Motivation will clearly underlie all programs in the partnership, as it does in all of education. There is a tendency on the part of those of us who have taught for many years, especially college faculty, to be skeptical and cynical about motivational theory and its application: it all seems so self-evident, so pedestrian, so elementary. Furthermore, there are certain causal factors that inhibit motivation—factors over which a teacher in a classroom can have little control. These include peer pressure, previous records of failure, competition from television and music, domestic difficulties, drugs, illness—and, at times, an irrelevant curriculum. Still, even as we recognize the interplay and interdependence of internal and external factors upon the school, even as we acknowledge that teaching is as much an art as a craft, we need to find ways of stimulating and encouraging all teachers, especially those who suffer from burnout or have grown cynical about motivational theory.

I have thus far concentrated on the motivation of students and teachers in the schools, but college faculty who have had to stimulate students or administrators who judge faculty for reappointment, promotion, and tenure recognize that the problem is at least as acute at institutions of higher learning. Certainly, we have developed more effective ways of judging than of motivating college teachers. Too few committees for the improvement of teaching (if they exist at all) are equal in force to the personnel committees that measure the quality of teaching for professional advancement. Yet an impressive body of literature has focused upon this issue: from Ericksen's *Motivation for Learning* (1974) and *The Essence of Good Teaching* (1984) and Eble's *Professors as Teachers* (1972), *The Craft of Teaching* (1976), and *The Aims of College Teaching* (1983) to Cross' *Beyond the Open Door* (1971) and *Accent on Learning* (1976). One of the key advantages of a partnership is that it makes elementary and secondary teachers self-conscious about the content of their classes and the college faculty sensitive to pedagogy and the ways in which they can improve student motivation. It reinforces the centrality of teaching and compensates for those aspects of teacher preparation that graduate schools have thus far largely neglected.

The goals that I have listed above had to be converted into practical programs between August 1983 and September 1988. A brief chronology of the main events will dramatically represent how a corporation, a group of school districts, and a college became an authentic educational partnership within four years. This chronology is included in Resource B. The following descriptions of programs for students, teachers, counselors, and leaders will illustrate how that partnership affected a large, heterogeneous community and formed novel associations and alliances.

6

Educational Programs
for Students

Programs offered directly to students present difficulties
for collaborations between colleges and schools. Since the sched-
uling of classes within a school system is necessarily restrictive,
especially for gifted students who are involved in many extracur-
ricular activities, any initiatives will have to be supplementary.
They have to be offered after school, in the evening, and during
the summer, and they must respect everyone's primary obligation to his or her home school.

The cooperation and leadership of superintendents are
especially important in any program for students. Superinten
dents provide the necessary support in underscoring the significance of work that reaches beyond the usual expectations.
Together with other partnership leaders, they can accomplish
a great deal for the highly motivated, the indifferent or unmotivated, and the at-risk student.

Gifted and Talented Students

Educational partnerships often concentrate initially on
these students because districts cannot afford to offer enough
programs for them. The students and their parents grow frustrated with the limited resources of small schools, even while
remaining pleased with the ability of these schools to offer personalized instruction. Small is better—sometimes; at other times
it can lead to serious limitations.

The recent emphasis on academic excellence and accelerated programs for the gifted has been driven by numerous educational reports and has translated itself politically into legislation by state education departments eager to restore standards. Rarely have rigorous requirements been so stressed by educators and politicians alike; rarely have programs for the gifted seemed so important to the future of the nation. When the search for excellence cannot be satisfied through individual school districts, the more extensive and flexible educational partnerships become an ideal structure.

The programs described in Chapter One have successfully provided services for gifted and talented students. These include the Advanced Placement Program, Syracuse University's Project Advance, and the Johns Hopkins Center for the Advancement of Academically Talented Youth. Beyond these proven national models, however, there are many other ways in which a local educational partnership can serve gifted students.

A very obvious alternative is to have high school seniors take college courses for credit. In the SUNY Purchase Westchester School Partnership, qualified seniors have been successfully integrated into the basic great books college course, "Revolutions in Western Thought." Since one major purpose of the course—in addition to having students read and write about the Bible, *The Republic, Dr. Faustus, The Communist Manifesto, The Origin of Species,* and other major texts of Western civilization—is to orient freshmen to college work, the same goal is especially attractive to high school seniors. Students get a head start on college subjects, they can use this experience in gaining entrance to their colleges of choice, and they can bring additional meaning to their senior year in high school. The college can go beyond this basic freshman course and make other courses in its general education program available to high school seniors. By doing so, it captures enrollments—often in subjects such as economics, psychology, or a foreign language that may not be offered in the high school—and develops a recruitment effort that is organic to its academic work. One should not be too cynical about these motives: partnerships, as John Goodlad has pointed out, generally proceed from enlightened self-interest.

There is a final benefit that a partnership can bring to programs for gifted and talented students. It can offer enrichment courses without removing students from their own schools. Advanced placement and Project Advance have been successful because they recognize that any initiative that disrupts the students' high school schedule will be resisted and will probably fail. There are countless examples of attempts to develop alternative public schools for the gifted, and some have been extraordinarily successful. The Boston Latin School is perhaps the most notable. Townsend Harris High School, associated with the City College of New York, was also rigorous and is remembered with affection (it is now linked to Queens College). Other New York schools—the Bronx High School of Science, Stuyvesant High School, and Hunter High School—also have distinguished heritages. There are many other public high schools that have served the gifted and talented—Ramsay Alternative High School, South Birmingham, Alabama; Chandler High School, Arizona; Roper School, Bloomfield Hills, Michigan; Governor's School, Charleston, South Carolina; Governor's School for the Gifted, Richmond, Virginia; Nile Kinnick High School, Seattle, Washington—but these were established at a time when public education was in a far healthier condition and not nearly so threatened by selective private and parochial schools.

Recently, efforts to develop alternative schools of excellence have met with strong resistance from leaders in local school districts. This was certainly true of Governor Mario Cuomo's effort to establish regional schools of excellence in New York State in 1985. Resistance to Cuomo's initiative grew almost entirely out of the self-interest of local school districts. In any case, some planning money was wasted, and an important initiative failed because it could not find an appropriate structure. But the impulse toward programs for gifted high school students should not be lost. An obvious alternative to a separate school is the college-school partnership. It allows students to remain in their own schools while offering them curricular opportunities that enrich the required course work.

Each partnership will undoubtedly develop programs appropriate to its school systems, but six generic types suggest how fruitful a partnership can be:

- In addition to the advanced placement courses that will continue to be offered through the schools, courses in less popular fields such as physics or classics should also be mounted; with numerous school districts participating, they become entirely feasible.
- High school seniors should be integrated into appropriate college courses in general education and the disciplines.
- An intensified core curriculum for half the day might be offered; it would supplement those high school requirements completed by students at their home school.
- A research opportunity program should be developed during the summer that will allow gifted science students to work at the research site of a university, hospital, or corporation; pursue a research project under the guidance of a mentor; and present a final report of findings. This program can be continued during the academic year so that a network of young researchers is developed.
- A science for students program could bring, on a continuing basis, classes of students to the college campus for intensive work in chemistry, biology, and ecology laboratories.
- A series of lectures and seminars in which business executives discuss career opportunities with high school juniors and seniors could be offered.

The structure of the partnership between colleges and schools makes these and other projects devoted to gifted and talented students relatively simple to implement. No programs within the partnership will create better relations with parents; none will be more popular.

Students at Risk

It is only natural that educational partnerships have been initiated as programs for gifted and talented students. Their parents have demanded services small districts cannot afford, and this pressure has been a major force behind the creation of college-school collaborations. But there is another side to this educational coin, reflecting another class of students that has no articulate, motivated, self-interested constituency arguing its case. I speak of dropouts and students at risk—those who may never graduate from high school. No college-school partnership can be complete without a program that deals with this educational underclass.

One of the major advantages that a collaboration between a college and schools has in helping at-risk students is that its programs can serve as reinforcement to whatever intervention strategy is used. The guidance counselor project and the Institute on Motivation are two obvious supportive activities. However, the workshops for effective leadership and the various institutes for teachers in the disciplines can also be partially addressed to students who are at risk in their schools. The programs of the partnership, which function autonomously and can be viewed as a series of vertical projects, also have lateral connections that become more manifest as the collaboration grows. Teachers, guidance counselors, and administrative leaders—all of whom have participated in the partnership—meet in their individual schools, where any program for at-risk students must finally be centered.

There is a growing number of dropout programs across the country: Project PATHE in Charleston, South Carolina; the Washington-Dix Street Academy in Washington, D.C., which is patterned after the "street academies" that developed in New York City in the 1960s; the Summer Training and Education Program in Philadelphia; the Youth Tutoring Project in San Antonio, Texas; the Postsecondary Planning Program in Dade County, Florida; the Adopt-a-Student Program in Atlanta, Georgia; and the Los Angeles Unified School District Dropout Recovery Prevention Program (Ranbom, 1986).

Three of the most valuable programs in terms of college-school collaborations are Cities in Schools, which is now headquartered in Washington, D.C.; the Middle College at LaGuardia Community College in New York City; and the Peer Leadership Development Program, which was organized in New Jersey in collaboration with the National Executive Service Corps. They are worth describing in some detail before we go on to consider how a dropout program can be most effectively integrated into an educational partnership.

Cities in Schools had its origins in the street academies that were established in the early 1960s in Harlem and the Lower East Side of New York as a form of alternative education for "at-risk youth, juvenile offenders, drug abusers, and aimless youth" (Milliken, 1986, p. 3). By 1973, the founders had set in place a model of an "integrated educational and social service delivery system" (p. 3) that they wished to replicate nationally. The *concept* consists of four elements:

- working partnerships between the public and private sectors for governing and funding the system
- the use of schools or alternative education sites as the field of action for the integrated delivery of human services
- repositioning of staff from existing human service agencies and volunteer organizations to avoid the need for infusions of new funds for better services
- the development of coordinating structures built around small, accountable, and personalized delivery units of transdisciplinary teams of teachers, social service professionals, and volunteers [Milliken, 1986, p. 3]

The *objectives* of a Cities in Schools project are to "improve at-risk students' school attendance; enhance their personal, educational, and social development; improve their employment attitudes and skills; increase parental involvement in their education; increase positive behavior and reduce encounters with the criminal justice system" (p. 4).

The *structure* in any city depends upon three sets of agreements: "an organizing committee . . . of leaders from the public and private sectors who *agree* to become the governing body of a CIS system; . . . a city director and two agency coordinators who secure *agreements* from human service agencies for the repositioning of staff in the school; and the education site project team, coordinated by a project director" who "works with small and manageable groups of students who, along with their parents, have formally *agreed* to participate in the system.'' Cities in Schools ''is a *process* that engages the entire community. It is a force to intervene creatively in the lives of students at high risk of failure while their education and employment options remain open. Repositioned human service providers are able to free teachers from some of the heaviest demands thrust on them by students troubled with nonschool problems. Teachers, social service providers, and volunteers find truly synergistic advantages as 'members of one orchestra playing in the same pit and from the same score''' (p. 4).

The Cities in Schools program is spreading rapidly, with regional centers in Pittsburgh and Los Angeles that provide consultation and technical assistance, as well as specific sites that range from West Palm Beach, Florida, and Bridgeport, Connecticut, to Houston, Texas, and Columbia, South Carolina. The present time is far more favorable to integrated human service systems than the 1960s, when the problems first surfaced, and governmental leaders have supported the growth of Cities in Schools.

A major claim of Cities in Schools is that the social service system intended to serve disadvantaged youth has been fragmented and competitive. The multibillion dollar war on poverty ''was characterized by a proliferation of programs and agencies which ultimately tended to serve the interests of the new middle class springing up around the organizations, rather than the poor'' (Milliken, 1986, p. 9). The leaders of Cities in Schools call for ''an alliance of private foundations and corporations, now becoming self-conscious stakeholders in public education, to help establish collaboration as the sine qua non in public education, and in the human enterprise, as well'' (p. 9).

Cities in Schools makes a compelling case, although sometimes their documents read like social sermons on the mount and their leaders come across as missionaries to the poor. In certain inner-city schools, the model has indeed worked, but it is not entirely compatible with the concept of an educational partnership and seems to be most effective within large cities where the problem of at-risk students is most acute.

Described as "a collaborative high school-college program directed to the needs of urban high school youth," the Middle College was established under the joint auspices of the New York City Board of Education and LaGuardia Community College of the City University of New York. The Middle College is an alternative high school that "admits prospective tenth-grade students, who have been identified by teachers and counselors, as high-risk youngsters with college potential" (Lieberman, 1986, p. 1). The model uses visible peer models, small classes, internships patterned after the college's cooperative education program, and the academic support services of the community college. The instructional programs are designed to meet the New York State Education Department requirements for a high school diploma in English, social studies, mathematics, science, music/art, language, and physical education. A key component is the career education/internship program. The guidance counselors arrange for nonpaying internships in community service agencies—hospitals, schools, police stations, and social service agencies. These internships are reinforced by seminars that serve as commentary on the work experience. Students can select internships from three categories—human services, business technology, and liberal arts and sciences—and receive credit toward their high school diploma.

Leaders of the Middle College attribute its success to a number of elements in the design of the internship program (Lieberman, 1986, p. 12):

- the three-year relationship maintained between individual students and their career education supervisors
- the careful placement of students in work environments that provide not only interesting work tasks but also co-workers and supervisors with whom students can interact positively
- close on-site monitoring of the students by the career education supervisors
- the staff's careful development of learning sites, which includes assessing the work-site climate and needs and communicating the school's goals to the work supervisor
- the reinforcement of the concepts acquired by students in and out of the classroom, through the seminar teaching

- the integrated nature of the experiential and academic learning, with mutual reinforcement
- the careful fit of the internship with the psychosocial needs of students to provide a source of purposefulness, pride, and self-worth and an external affirmation of the students' ability to function in a world previously perceived as unrewarding, hostile, and uncaring

Compared to a dropout rate of 40 percent in New York City high schools, Middle College has a rate of only 15 percent. One would naturally expect a much greater degree of success, given the support systems put into place, but even so the figures are impressive, and they seem to confirm that the "combination of cooperative education and small classes is a winning strategy" (Lieberman, 1986, p. 15).

Our own partnership drew upon various aspects of Cities in Schools, the Middle College, and other programs. We initiated an at-risk program in New Rochelle, one of the communities closest to New York City, with the intention of replicating it in other partnership school districts. As in the Middle College, our concentration was on the tenth grade. We selected twenty-five volunteer students who were at least two grades below level in basic skills and had negative feelings about school or showed signs that they would probably drop out. An important condition was that the parents agree to participate in the program by attending meetings designed to orient them to school practices and to show them new ways of helping their children with their education.

The program was individualized for each student by setting up a team that included a mentor who gave personal advice and support to the student, tutors in school subjects, a social worker, a coordinating teacher who was designated as a site director, and regular school staff as needed. Remedial work in basic subjects, preemployment guidance, and help in finding summer or after-school jobs were also available. Students with hobbies and special talents were encouraged to develop them.

Several elements are essential if a program of this type is to succeed. As Cities in Schools has demonstrated, there must be active involvement by city officials, support from the super-

intendent of schools and the board of education, and leadership from the heads of social service agencies and businesses
in the community. Cities in Schools insists that individuals from
these agencies must form a governing board that will make final
decisions about the program, but the structure of a college-school
collaboration will not allow it. A governing board of this kind
is surely crucial for success, but it must remain advisory to the
policy-making steering committee of the partnership. This does
not mean that the advisory committee will not be a powerful
influence in shaping the program. But ultimate authority must
remain with the steering committee of superintendents and college administrators so that the necessary checks and balances
will remain in place and there will be a sense of proportion
among programs. The steering committee has a comprehensive view of the entire partnership and can prevent a single program from assuming excessive autonomy or independence.

Our own program promises to be highly successful in the
city of New Rochelle, and we now have plans to extend these
activities to other school districts in the partnership. Some of
this success is deceptive. Any program with so much individualized attention and supplementary support ought to have a considerable measure of success, but it is equally true that no other
approach will work with at-risk students. The common elements
of the best programs are clear: strong support from the superintendent, principal, and other administrators; the active endorsement of municipal leaders; the presence of repositioned
staff from social agencies on the school site; the cooperation of
parents; direct linkage of the school with work internships; the
continuing attempt to personalize the program and thus lend
the vulnerable student constant psychological help; and consis-
tent monitoring of the student's behavior.

The added feature that an educational partnership brings
to an at-risk program is really an extension and reinforcement
of all these elements. It can establish a set of activities that incorporates the finest dimensions of the most successful programs,
and, at the same time, it can connect those activities with others
in the partnership. Most at-risk enterprises are forms of alternative education and are set aside from the ongoing events of
the school. By having teaching institutes in various disciplines,

guidance counselor externships, a leadership center for administrators, a program in motivation that keeps those administrators and their teachers aware of how to motivate traditional as well as at-risk students, by integrating the gifted and talented (who are, after all, role models) into college classes, by including retired executives and community volunteers into all partnership activities—by making connections among all of these programs and having them vital and active, as further reinforcement for at-risk students, the chances of success are considerably enhanced. An at-risk program depends upon the concept of partnership and can only be buttressed by the larger educational partnership to which it is wedded.

One program that attempts to offer a partial solution to the problems of at-risk students will illustrate how all the programs in a partnership interact and reinforce each other. The Peer Leadership Development Program was developed at Princeton High School in 1980 by Sharon Rose Powell, a psychologist, and has spread to six New Jersey urban high schools. Its purpose is to "help freshmen adjust to their new environment by providing support from upperclass students, [and it] includes an intensive training course in group dynamics and leadership techniques for upperclass peer-group leaders. It also includes regular group discussions with freshmen about such issues as social and academic pressures; relationships with peers, parents, and faculty; and problems associated with drugs, sex, and alcohol" (Powell, 1987, p. 1).

The peer leaders, carefully selected to serve as role models for the younger students, take a seminar for credit and learn about problem solving, leadership techniques, adolescent psychology, and group dynamics. This seminar has seven objectives (Powell, 1987, p. 5):

1. to help students understand their own value structure and how their values affect relationships with other people
2. to help students think through problems and explore alternatives
3. to help students develop an awareness of the processes which occur as a group develops

4. to help students examine different leadership
    styles
5. to help students learn how to facilitate the ac-
    tive participation of all members in the group
6. to help students learn how to encourage cohe-
    sion and cooperation in a group
7. to help students improve communication skills

The Peer Leadership Development Program has now been replicated in three high schools in Brooklyn and in Dobbs Ferry, Port Chester, and the Tarrytowns in Westchester County. It rests on the crucial elements of role modeling and mentoring and, most importantly, on the need for young people to *belong* to new groups they join. It deals with at-risk freshmen, but it is clearly concerned with guidance, motivation, and of course leadership. It draws strength from these other programs in the partnership and has a much greater chance for success because of its association with them.

7

Professional Development Programs for Teachers

Most successful partnerships concentrate on training schoolteachers in their individual disciplines. The pedagogical implementation of subject matter ultimately rests with the teachers themselves, and the best service that a partnership can perform is to provide as much information as possible. But the teachers are keenly interested in classroom strategies, too, and thus a format must be found through which the discrete strengths of college faculty and schoolteachers complement each other—faculty providing a deeper knowledge of the subject and teachers the pedagogy that will work in their classrooms. For example, the Bay Area Writing Project has developed into the National Writing Project and has been successful in training teachers in composition; Syracuse University's Project Advance has worked well by using a variation of advanced placement and having high school teachers handle more sophisticated subject matter in their own classrooms; the National Faculty makes it possible for college faculty to work with high school teachers on their own turf; the Yale–New Haven Teachers Institute has college and high school faculty share teaching strategies in addition to acquiring knowledge of the subject; and the Academic Alliances program rests upon ''local communities of inquiry in the disciplines.''

All these programs, described in Chapter One, are effective in their particular ways and deserve to be adapted or modified to local needs. But from the perspective of a comprehensive educational partnership that includes all levels of education, as well as corporations, the community, and governmental agencies, the Woodrow Wilson National Fellowship Foundation Program is most appropriate. Rooted in peer teaching, it offers teachers the opportunity to continue their professional interest in a discipline. This organic approach to teacher training has thus far succeeded remarkably well in training and retraining thousands of teachers in chemistry, mathematics, and physics and is now offering an institute in writing. The model can be adapted, as we will see, to all disciplines in the curriculum and even to the motivation of teachers. It can also be associated with the research projects of college faculty and engage high school and college students as interns to those projects. The model is extremely flexible, but at its core is peer teaching, developed at Princeton University in the sciences and now replicated in thirty sites across the country.

Mathematics and Science

The Woodrow Wilson National Fellowship Foundation Institutes are a direct response to the national anxiety about poor science education that is a central feature of *A Nation at Risk* (National Commission, 1983) and other recent reports. Reform is possible because of exemplary teachers who have discovered what will work in the classroom and who want to communicate this practical knowledge to their colleagues. When peer teaching is well organized, it is still the most effective way to improve classroom instruction.

The benefits of teachers teaching teachers at the same level of instruction need to be underscored. The format engenders mutual respect and reinforces the significance of teaching through exemplary instructors who share experiences with their peers. It encourages rapid and efficient transmission of knowledge and leads to an interaction between teachers who may previously have been intellectually isolated in separate schools. It recreates the intellectual excitement that formed a large part of their initial desire to become teachers; it promotes collegiality among teachers at a time when their profession is under attack; it frees teaching from bureaucratic constraints and regulations; and it recognizes master teachers as first among equals.

The model developed by the Woodrow Wilson National Fellowship Foundation is worth emulating. As with most programs, the inspiration stemmed from a highly motivated and gifted person, Amie Knox, who had spent her career as a teacher of science and a school administrator in Connecticut and had also served as an educational consultant to the Woodrow Wilson Foundation. The director of planning and development for the foundation, Caroline Wilson, worked with Knox in raising funds and administering the program. The "master teacher program for high school mathematics and science teachers" originated in 1982 with a series of summer institutes, largely funded by the Camille and Henry Dreyfus Foundation, that brought together the finest chemistry and mathematics teachers in the country. For four weeks, fifty teachers studied under nationally recognized scientists, examined the latest developments in their fields, and then produced curricular materials that they knew would be effective. These materials were published by the foundation and disseminated by teachers to groups of their colleagues. At the end of the summer institutes held at Princeton University, Woodrow Wilson Foundation administrators selected exceptional teachers from the group of fifty and formed teams of four teachers who went to different sites, mostly college campuses, to teach local high school teachers in one-week "mini-institutes."

Our own partnership was able to adopt the Woodrow Wilson model within the first year of our existence and become a satellite of the national program. The one-week intensive mini-institutes in chemistry and statistics were self-selected by teachers in our community. As a consequence, they attracted highly motivated educators, some of whom returned in subsequent summers. More than 80 percent had master's degrees. Many were women who had graduated from Radcliffe, Brown, Smith, Bryn Mawr, and Vassar, and had returned to teaching after raising their families. These were experienced teachers who were involved with the full range of chemistry and math courses in their home school. Since, in many cases, the districts had paid for their registration, they carried with them a certain sense of institutional obligation. Others paid their own tuition and were self-motivated, while still others sought in-service or graduate credit for their participation. The educator's dream was realized: master teachers, trained at the Woodrow Wilson Foundation, worked with knowledgeable colleagues who wanted and needed to learn more about their subject.

The Woodrow Wilson program has flourished because it depends on the simple concept of teachers teaching teachers. The concentration is on the classroom and what will work there. But it has also been able to grow rapidly and at the same time maintain extremely high standards of excellence because it has encouraged decentralization. In the summer of 1985 there were eleven sites for the teaching of chemistry, mathematics, and other scientific subjects; in 1986, the number had grown to twenty-one; in 1987 there were twenty-nine sites hosting thirty-nine mini-institutes. As the administrators of the program point out, "The people who attended were particularly receptive to being taught by their peers; they understood one another and could share teaching strategies and other common concerns. The ratio of four teachers to thirty participants allowed for extra help in labs and with computers. In fact, many reported this experience to be the most valuable of their academic lives. Reunions at follow-up workshops during the winter consolidated the group and led to requests for more involvement" (Knox, 1986, p. 3). The impact of the program is awesome. "In 1986, such an expanded program [of thirty teachers in thirty-nine mini-institutes] could reach 900 local schoolteachers. If, as commonly assumed, each teacher has 100 students, 90,000 students would therefore benefit" (p. 3).

At our own campus, our professor of chemistry, Carlo Parravano, functioned as director of the project and later became leader of all precollegiate science education; he provided the environment and setting in which the Woodrow Wilson teachers could flourish. Although he did not teach any of the workshops—the success of the program depends upon peer teaching—he was constantly present as a resource person, interacting with the teachers informally to create an ambience in which instruction would prosper and offering an occasional lecture on a subject such as the scientific method. By the end of the first summer's program, he had decided to encourage his colleagues to be present when the next Woodrow Wilson mini-institutes were in session so that there would be even more contact between college and school faculty.

The program is pragmatic and unpretentious. While the teachers are eager to hear speakers on the topic under discussion, and they do not need, for the purposes of this institute, college faculty lecturing them on material they already know. But conversations at coffee breaks, cocktail hours, and after the sessions themselves—held in the natural science building, where the college faculty pursue their own research—are invaluable.

Decentralization of the program encourages its continuation throughout the academic year, a vital condition for long-range success. The teachers in our community returned for five follow-up sessions, organized once again by our professor of chemistry and taught by the Woodrow Wilson master teachers. A network was soon created that allowed the teachers to share up-to-date information through subsequent meetings, through a newsletter, and through whatever friendships developed. This interaction provides the most invaluable dimension of the entire project, for it fosters a sense of pride and collegiality at a time when the teaching profession is undergoing severe criticism, and it confirms the importance of quality instruction by having the master teachers as leaders. Because the program uses the college campus as a setting and a professor of chemistry as project director, the teachers feel reaffirmed in their own disciplines.

Within our college partnership, the Woodrow Wilson Institutes became a model of how to communicate directly with teachers. The summer of 1985 brought fifty-seven teachers into chemistry and statistics mini-institutes; by 1986, there were four institutes of thirty teachers each—chemistry, mathematics, physics, and a locally developed earth science institute. In 1987, eight mini-institutes featured these four disciplines, introduced a writing mini-institute, and repeated chemistry, mathematics, and physics for New York City teachers. We projected extended summer institutes of our own to train master teachers in fields that the Woodrow Wilson National Fellowship Foundation was not considering—biology, psychology, economics, political science, history, writing/literature and foreign languages. We would thus create a training program patterned after the Woodrow Wilson Institutes. Our college faculty began to work with master teachers throughout the metropolitan community.

The next step, which is also a natural extension of the Woodrow Wilson Fellowship program, is to develop institutes for elementary and middle school teachers. The members of science and math departments often feel distant from the special needs of elementary teachers, who themselves are far more comfortable with literature and the arts, have little knowledge of math and science, and suffer from an understandable anxiety when the subjects are introduced. Fortunately, we had established a Teachers Center under the sponsorship of the State Education Department. This center, which became associated with the partnership in 1985, concentrates on elementary mathematics and science. The center is autonomous and has a twenty-one-person policy board, composed of a majority of teachers as well as several college faculty, school and college administrators, and community leaders; it is closely allied to our partnership. It is located in the natural science building so that a continuum in math and science education has been established that runs from elementary school to college. In collaboration with the Teachers Center, elementary and middle school teachers will be trained through our Center for Mathematics and Science by gifted high school teachers who have already been trained themselves in the Woodrow Wilson Institutes. The ideal is to have trained elementary teachers working with their own peers. At this point, however, they have had no formal training in any of the sciences, they seek direction, and it seems wisest to have the guidance come from those on the next level of schooling, namely, high school teachers of mathematics and science.

Most elementary teachers have had little formal training in science and do not have the resources to improve their knowledge or skills. College-level texts and courses are rarely appropriate, and the resource materials accompanying elementary school science books and activity kits are not adequate. Too often, the teacher responds by neglecting science in the classroom. Our first effort was to hold a series of Saturday workshops for elementary teachers. Now we plan to develop two-week summer institutes similar in design to those that have been so successful with high school teachers. They will be structured around a series of workshops, each emphasizing a specific curriculum unit. According to the director of our Center for Mathematics and Science Education, Carlo Parravano (1987, p. 26):

> The workshops will be designed to enable teachers to perform numerous science activities successfully and to add to their conceptual understanding of the science topics involved. In addition, this program will attempt to instill elementary schoolteachers with a spirit of inquiry and an enthusiasm for science that they will carry over into the classroom.
>
> Curriculum and materials for the institutes will be planned at SUNY Purchase by a K-2 team, a 3-4 team, and a 5-6 team, each consisting of a local high school science teacher and two elementary school master teachers. The work of the teams would be coordinated by a science curriculum coordinator, an individual qualified in elementary science teacher training.
>
> During the first year, the teams will spend four weeks planning the summer institutes. Science topics consistent with the recently mandated New York State Elementary Science Syllabus would be developed by each team. The institute's curriculum will include, for each of the topics selected:
>
> 1. a background lecture on the scientific content
> 2. an array of demonstrations and student activities to illustrate the topic
> 3. an examination of relevant computer software
> 4. a discussion of ways to incorporate science into other areas of the curriculum, such as writing, reading, mathematics, and art

Each team will develop a series of modular elementary science units that are relatively easy for teachers to use and that do not require large amounts of teacher preparation time. Each module will include an activity kit, the instructional materials, supplies, and apparatus needed to investigate a particular science topic, plus clearly defined lesson plans.

During each of the next two years, two weeklong summer institutes will be offered for twenty K–2 teachers, twenty 3–4 teachers, and twenty 5–6 teachers. The planning team will serve as a faculty, presenting the materials they have developed. The format will include a combination of lectures, demonstrations, and classroom activities.

As with the high school teacher institutes, follow-up activities are a vital component of a successful program:

Four follow-up sessions will be held during the school year following the summer institute. Participants will be expected to use some of the classroom materials early in the school year and be prepared to discuss their effectiveness with the institute faculty at the first follow-up session. The three subsequent follow-up sessions open to institute participants as well as other teachers in the community will introduce new science topics and activities presented by guest science teachers or members of the institute faculty. . . .

By the end of the two weeklong institutes, each elementary schoolteacher will have been exposed to topics in both the physical and life sciences, explored the scientific background for each unit, performed activities based on this unit, and tailored the lesson plans provided to their own needs. A follow-up session will focus on the effectiveness of the teaching materials and successful teaching strategies that individual teachers employ to incorporate them. Additional follow-up sessions will provide participating teachers with new science materials supplementing what was presented in the summer institutes [Parravano, 1987, p. 27].

These self-contained training institutes and the mini-institutes led by the Woodrow Wilson Foundation, together with our association with the Teachers Center, form the core of our Center for Mathematics and Science Education. Other elements augment teacher training: research opportunities for teachers and students, residential teaching fellowships, programs for minorities and women, a consultant board that serves school districts, and special conferences on the teaching of modern physics and other subjects.

We feel that for these highly qualified and gifted teachers there is the clear need and keen desire to go beyond the summer institutes. Hence, we wish to establish a program for mathematics and science teachers who, like their counterparts teaching at the university level, can profit from the professional stimulation of a research experience. This program will offer summer research opportunities to experienced high school science and mathematics teachers, placing them with a research group at a local university or industrial research center under the mentorship of a research scientist. Performing research is a vital aspect of any instructional program and a leading force in college and graduate programs; yet, opportunities for secondary school teachers to pursue research under the guidance of the finest teachers and laboratory scientists are virtually nonexistent in most teacher enhancement programs. Working in a research environment enables teachers to develop problem-solving skills, a broader scientific background, intellectual flexibility, good work habits, clear communication skills, and the ability to work with others in solving difficult problems; important traits to be transmitted to students. . . .

In close proximity are numerous corporate

headquarters and research centers (IBM Watson
Laboratory, Union Carbide, CIBA-Geigy, General
Foods, Stauffer, and so on) medical research facilities (Sloan-Kettering, Albert Einstein, Mt. Sinai),
and major research universities (Yale, New York,
and Columbia universities; Lamont-Doherty Geo-
physical Observatory, and so on). SUNY Purchase
is also well suited to serve as a central site for this
program. The college faculty has in the past informally collaborated with secondary schoolteachers
and students on research projects, and the performance of research with undergraduates is an important component of the college's curriculum. As
a result, the college faculty has valuable experience
defining and supervising an appropriate research
experience and would serve as ideal mentors [Par-
ravano, 1987, p. 28].

By participating in ongoing projects of college faculty
members or research mentors in corporate and hospital laboratories, the teachers will engage in sponsored research that is
virtually guaranteed publication. They will avoid expensive,
time-consuming start-up periods and help to create a research-
team spirit. Finally, exposure to sophisticated researchers will
inevitably improve their teaching and give them a sense of be-
longing to a profession rather than only performing a job. As
Parravano (1987) notes:

This program would select twelve high school
teachers from the metropolitan New York region
and match each with a research mentor. Each high
school teacher will spend eight weeks during the
summer working at the research site. An important component of this program will be weekly
evening seminars held during the summer which
will permit the high school teachers to describe their
research to one another, explore ways in which the
research experience can improve the quality of their

teaching, and establish a special esprit de corps
nurtured by their shared research experience. Following the summer research experience, the teachers will be expected to work with their mentors
preparing a written report on their research. This
report will form the basis for a presentation at an
institute follow-up session at the center. The participating teachers will also be expected to speak
about their research to groups of interested high
school students and make advisory suggestions to
students participating in science fairs. In addition,
one teacher per year will be selected and funded
to make a presentation of his or her research results
at a meeting of the appropriate professional society [p. 29].

The Center for Mathematics and Science Education is
now funded significantly by the National Science Foundation
for four years, with supplementary support from IBM. In addition to the institutes for elementary and secondary teachers
and the research opportunities for high school teachers, it includes a conference on the teaching of modern physics, science
colloquia for teachers, a consultant board of science teachers
available to local districts, and strategies for dissemination and
replication throughout the densely populated New York metropolitan area. With the imprimatur of the National Science Foundation, the possibilities for further support from local corporations such as IBM become greatly enhanced. One of the
programs we wish to pursue is Research Opportunities for High
School Students, adapted from our own project for high school
teachers and from the Hyman Rickover program for extremely
gifted students that was so successful in Leesburg, Virginia.
Another feature that could develop from the math/science institutes is a SUNY Purchase residential teaching fellowship, which
would provide the opportunity for teachers to immerse themselves for an academic year in a college environment. A screen-
ing process could produce teachers who join a department,
take courses, participate in seminars, conduct research with

colleagues, supervise student projects, and prepare curriculum materials of use to them when they return to their high schools. This leave of absence could be invaluably restorative to the teachers, at the same time as the department enjoys the presence and activity of a visiting, intensely motivated teacher. Lamentably, the idea will be difficult to realize through the budgets of small school districts—that one chemistry teacher in a high school of 400 students is indispensable—and we will need to seek foundation support for a residential teaching fellowship that can become highly selective and prestigious. It is too good an idea to surrender to constraining budgets.

Finally, any Center for Mathematics and Science Education must include a program for minorities and female students. An impressive activity that engages high school minority students in science is conducted at the City College of New York and one for girls in elementary school has been developed at Wesleyan College. Arnold Strassenburg, director of the Division of Teacher Preparation and Enhancement at the National Science Foundation, expresses the widespread view that it is critical to reach students, especially girls and minorities, at the elementary and middle-school level. By the time they reach high school, many students have already made a decision about whether they will pursue an interest in the sciences. That interest can be stimulated in the classroom, as we have indicated in our discussion of the institutes for elementary teachers, but in the end the best way is probably through a variety of activities and special events that make mathematics and science fun rather than forbidding.

These different dimensions—the one- or two-week mini-institutes for secondary and elementary teachers, the four-week institutes to train master teachers, the teacher research opportunities, the conferences on teaching modern science, the consultant board of science teachers, and the residential teaching fellowships—have evolved into a Science Center that requires supplies, equipment, laboratory assistants, and coherent leadership. Because of the programmatic support from the private sector, we were able to persuade the State University of New York to fund two lines for the science director and his administrative assistant. The funding interaction between the private and public sectors, between a company such as IBM and the State University of New York produces powerful leverage as one challenges the other. Private funding persuades the university that its support is warranted and university resources give confidence to industry and business. With the support now given by the National Science Foundation, that effect will be greatly intensified, as we seek funding for student programs that the foundation does not underwrite because of the self-imposed limitations of its teacher enhancement guidelines.

All these efforts, under the leadership of the science director, have been reinforced by an advisory committee composed of the finest teachers of science in both public and private schools throughout the community. Their role in shaping the future of the Center for Mathematics and Science is central as they divide themselves into subcommittees concerned with curriculum, research, teaching strategies, special events, and so on. They also serve as a constant reminder to the superintendents and the school boards of how valuable the partnership is to their school districts. Needless to say, a proposal to any foundation has an unimpeachable authority when such teachers guarantee its importance.

The appointment of a science director and an administrative assistant through state funding has given the Science Center a sense of solidity and permanence. It has also identified two people who are employed full-time, not only administering the program of the center but developing further grant support. Wherever possible, we request technical assistance, supplies, and equipment, all of which reside permanently in the natural science building and supplement a traditionally austere state budget. Very early in the process, the science faculty saw that support was more forthcoming in this way than through the state budget, and they embraced the partnership as their own. As they watch more than 300 motivated science teachers in summer institutes and numerous follow-up sessions during the year, as their advice is sought, and as they participate in these various activities, they become organically part of the collaboration between college and schools.

It is important to return, as a concluding note, to the centrality of the teacher. All of us must serve the teacher as he or she in turn serves his or her students. Ways must be found to keep teachers professionally *au courant,* to create connections between them and others in their disciplines, to return them to college campuses where research is being conducted, to help them improve their classroom performance. Many of the efforts that I have described in Chapter One engage teachers in some of these ways; but of all the models I have observed, the one developed by the Woodrow Wilson Foundation is most effective for the training of teachers. Its success is directly connected to an uncompromising demand for excellence: only the finest teachers are selected to attend the institutes on the Princeton University campus. Exemplary teachers are chosen from this group to be part of a four-person team that offers a mini-institute. Because they respect the master teachers of the institutes and the entire program so much, local teachers are eager to attend the mini-institutes and the follow-up sessions during the year. The Woodrow Wilson National Fellowship Foundation Program— both its four-week institutes and one-week mini-institutes— deserve to be replicated broadly by other colleges, partnerships, and school districts throughout the country. The adaptations that we have made in our partnership are but one example of how a core concept of teacher training can grow into a Center for Mathematics and Science Education.

The Woodrow Wilson Institutes have been successful because they engage the best and brightest administrators and teachers in their disciplines and implement the latest trends in curriculum development. In focusing initially on the sciences, the institutes have attempted to improve instruction on those levels where guidance is especially important, and they have grown rapidly because the disciplines of chemistry, mathematics, and physics are so clearly defined. Pedagogical implementation has been built upon the security of disciplines that have historically existed in the high schools and colleges; now the need is to reach into the elementary and middle schools as well. The model can and should be extended throughout the curriculum.

In the next three sections, I have selected disciplines in

which our own partnership implemented teachers institutes—economics, foreign languages, and esthetics. Each of them has its own inherent needs and special configuration, but the concept of teachers teaching teachers is their common center.

Social Sciences: Economics

If the current state of science education is somewhat questionable, instruction in economics is even more primitive. We are just beginning to realize and recognize how little students know about U.S. economic institutions and their relationship to the world's monetary systems and how vital such knowledge is to their well-being. If students do not learn how our free economic system works, if they do not come to understand why so many Third-World nations remain underdeveloped, and if they remain ignorant of the issues involved in consumerism, savings, and investment, they will be unprepared as voters and citizens to make the free choices essential to a democracy.

The problem is clearly too vast for any single organization to resolve, but the Joint Council of Economic Education (JCEE) is certainly making a courageous effort. It has established a nationwide network of 50 affiliated state councils and 270 university-based centers for economic education, and it has also set up a process called the Developmental Economic Education Program (DEEP), which has an elaborate support system for school districts that includes "instructional materials, effective teacher training, and professional service by local economic educators at all grade levels. *In those school systems where there is an active DEEP economic educational effort, students score one to two grade levels higher on tests of economic understanding*" (JCEE, 1986, p. 3). This result is scarcely surprising since "DEEP's approach is to work with an entire school system, introducing teachers and students to economics in a logical fashion, starting early in a child's learning experience and continuing throughout the grade levels and curriculum" (p. 5).

Another element that has contributed greatly to the success of DEEP has been the Joint Council's recognition that no educational program of this scope can prosper without the collaboration of community agencies—business, labor, government, and parent groups as well as educational institutions. The national organization, with a board of directors that includes leaders representing these different constituencies, has its statewide organizations, which in turn have eclectic boards of directors that monitor DEEP activities and support them through active fund raising.

Our own experience in the SUNY Purchase Westchester School Partnership may be typical. When we expressed an interest in becoming affiliated with the New York State Council on Economic Education, the response of Michael MacDowell, president of JCEE, and Sanford Gordon, executive director of the New York State Council, was immediately encouraging and free of bureaucratic entanglements. Once the director of our Economic Center was named in November 1985—a professor of economics, Peter Bell, at SUNY Purchase—and a plan for working with our school districts was approved by early 1986, the state council endorsed SUNY Purchase as an Economics Center in New York State by March, and then furnished funding that allowed us to conduct an Economics Institute in July 1986. In formulating our own plans—Bell found it extremely useful to have a curriculum specialist in a local high school system work as his associate—we were overwhelmed by the response from teachers. More than forty teachers answered our announcements of the program. They obviously felt not only the responsibility and the need to know economics but the desire as well.

That response was triggered by several forces. The State Education Department had stated its intention to impose a high school graduation requirement by 1989 that every student complete a one-semester course in economics. There was the inevitable discussion by many high school administrators and teachers of how to circumvent the regulation through a proficiency examination that might serve as an equivalency. Superintendents and teachers sought to preserve current electives, with all their vested interests, and viewed this new requirement as competitive. But at the same time teachers recognized the need to teach students economics so that they would be better prepared to understand world problems largely shaped and controlled by economics. The teachers also realized that little in their own background prepared them to teach economics. In our survey of 113 high school teachers in the partnership districts—and these included some of the best paid and best educated teachers in the country—60 percent had fewer than six credits of college economics and 86 percent had fewer than six graduate credits. The combination of the state regulation and the teachers' independent need and desire to know more economics created a demand for training that we could scarcely satisfy.

The JCEE has voluminous materials for the training of teachers in economics. The key document is a master curriculum guide entitled *A Framework for Teaching the Basic Concepts*. First published in 1977, "it provided the foundation for a series of *Teaching Strategies* that demonstrate how to introduce the conceptual framework of economics at various grade levels" (Mac-Dowell, 1984). By 1987 seven strategies had been published, the curriculum guide had gone through a revised edition, a television/film series ("Trade Off" and "Give and Take") based on the guide was available, and a library of DEEP materials assisted "in curriculum revision and in-service training of teachers" (Saunders, 1984, p. 11). The entire enterprise, as stated in the Preface to the *Framework*, "reflects the heavy emphasis on economics as a way of thinking rather than a set of answers, which was contained in the *Report of the National Task Force on Economic Education*, published in 1961." That report was "the first systematic effort by distinguished economists and teachers to give direction and shape to economics education in grades K–12." Throughout the sixties and seventies a great many economics educators and teachers developed curriculum materials and organized a set of twenty-two fundamental economics concepts upon which teacher training is based (p. 11):

Fundamental Economic Concepts

1. Scarcity
2. Opportunity Cost and Trade-Offs
3. Productivity

4. Economic Systems
5. Economic Institutions and Incentives
6. Exchange, Money, and Interdependence

Microeconomic Concepts

7. Markets and Prices
8. Supply and Demand
9. Competition and Market Structure
10. Income Distribution
11. Market Failures
12. The Role of Government

Macroeconomic Concepts

13. Gross National Product
14. Aggregate Supply
15. Aggregate Demand
16. Unemployment
17. Inflation and Deflation
18. Monetary Policy
19. Fiscal Policy

International Economic Concepts

20. Absolute and Comparative Advantage and Barriers to Trade
21. Balance of Payments and Exchange Rates
22. International Aspects of Growth and Stability

These concepts are explicated in the curriculum guide and can form the basis for any teacher training center in economics, for they constitute a fundamental approach to the discipline. In our case, we drew upon the full resources of the JCEE and developed a teachers institute that was structurally similar to the math/science institutes of the Woodrow Wilson National Fellowship Foundation Program. Unlike those institutes, however, we could not simply bring trained teachers of chemistry, statistics, physics, and earth science on to our campus to teach their own peers. Economics was not a clearly defined discipline in the schools, with teachers who had undergraduate degrees

waiting simply for retraining. We needed to return to funda-
mentals, to train master teachers, to create with the help of the
Joint Council's materials a discipline that could fit into the current curriculum.

Our first weeklong Economics Institute attracted forty
social science teachers. It divided the day into two parts. In the
morning, the director discussed economics as a distinct social
science and offered a broad view of the major issues that had
to be included in any economics course. The afternoon was
devoted to a discussion of pedagogy led by the associate director. We will have to repeat this process for several years until
we can choose master teachers similar to those trained by the
Woodrow Wilson National Fellowship Foundation.

Humanities: Foreign Languages

If a fundamental intention of partnerships between colleges and schools is to create coherence and integration in education, instruction in the humanities must inevitably inform that
intention. If ours is a culture of separation, in which educators
at different levels of learning do not always communicate with
one another, the humanities must insist that all participants in
the educational partnership stress the primacy of language instruction, invoke the significance of past cultures, make the
disciplinary connections that would otherwise be absent, and
underscore the ethical and civic dimensions that may tend to
be forgotten. These dimensions, which begin in the privacy of
the individual mind, must ultimately emerge, as Ladner has
pointed out, into a community of discourse that fosters thinking not only as an isolated, private activity but also as convivial,
collective public deliberation. This is the concern for civility—
"those cooperative efforts which ensure the care of the public
realm in which we all exist" (Ladner, 1984, p. 5).

The greatest single benefactor of the humanities within
the past twenty years has surely been the National Endowment
for the Humanities. Its seminar program involving distinguished
faculty and selected teachers has proven to be enormously successful. By now scores of teachers have met at universities for

revitalization in the humanities, usually concentrating on a specific author.

In response to the development of college-school collaborations, the National Endowment for the Humanities has lent major seed support to the National Writing Project at Berkeley, the National Humanities Faculty, and the Yale–New Haven Teachers Institute. Within the category Humanities Instruction in Elementary and Secondary Schools, it has established Institutes for Teachers and Administrators, which "consist of four weeks of intensive summer study on a college or university campus"; Collaborative Projects, which take place over a period of several years; and Summer Humanities Programs for High School Students at Historically Black Colleges and Universities, which "bring promising high school students" to those institutions. The institutes are extremely varied: "Teaching Shakespeare" at the Folger Shakespeare Library; "Vergil's *Aeneid*" at Miami University in Oxford, Ohio; "The Age of Franklin Roosevelt, 1929–45" at Bard College; "Islam: Religion, Culture, and History" at Princeton, New Jersey; "The American Constitution" at the California State University in Los Angeles; a Summer Institute for Precollegiate Instructors in French at SUNY Potsdam; the Providence-Brown Teaching Project at Brown University, which runs three-week summer institutes, "preceded by four afternoon seminars in the spring and followed by five evening seminars in the fall," which includes such topics as "comedies and tragedies of Shakespeare, the industrial revolution, and Latin American culture and literature"; and Partners in Education at Princeton University, a three-year project that emphasizes meetings throughout the academic year following a four-week summer institute devoted to such subjects as "(1) nineteenth-century American thought, (2) literature of North and South America, and (3) important philosophical and political concepts in the humanities" (National Endowment for the Humanities, 1986, pp. 3–33).

The support of the National Endowment for the Humanities has been extremely important to the study of the humanities at all levels of education and, as noted in Chapter One, the endowment has been responsible for two major collaborations: the

National Humanities Faculty and the National Writing Project. Partnerships should integrate activities of the endowment into their programs as appropriate. The Academic Alliance Movement has also strengthened individual disciplines. One of the most successful alliances has been in foreign languages, now represented at thirty different sites across the country.

Our own effort to promote the study of the humanities has been to make local adaptations of the Woodrow Wilson Fellowship Program. In foreign languages, for example, a college instructor has shaped a one-week institute in the summer and follow-up sessions during the academic year in collaboration with a large group of high school teachers. The teachers have been worried about the new state regulations that insist that students demonstrate oral competency because the teachers themselves are not altogether fluent in the foreign language. The summer institute has two parts—morning sessions during which techniques such as James Asher's "total physical response," Krashen and Tarrel's "natural approach," and Caleb Gattegno's "silent way" are presented, and afternoon workshops when the teachers work with their own leaders to see how these pedagogical methods as well as new curricular developments can be integrated into their classrooms. A final day is devoted to language and culture. We have received some support from the Economic Education Security Act, which provides flow-through money from the federal to the state government, and we have set registration at $160 for each of the thirty teachers enrolled. With these funds, a Foreign Language Institute has been born.

The enthusiastic teachers who comprise the planning committee of the Foreign Language Institute have indicated how the state regulations can be realistically adapted in their schools; and, from this committee, leaders have inevitably emerged—those who will be the local variation of the nationally selected Woodrow Wilson master teachers. While our approach is inductive and lacks the broad perspective of the Woodrow Wilson program, it has the benefit of growing from within our community and of empowering local teachers. It also fortifies the entire partnership as these teachers interact with their colleagues and administrators. As the foreign language project grows, we will be developing a proposal that includes an extensive program for international studies and a language laboratory to serve not only the college but the partnership districts as well. The necessary supplies and equipment—computers, video and music tapes, art books, and reproductions—will be permanently established on our campus for use by our own students. The chances of funding a language laboratory will of course be infinitely greater if we reach out to the larger community rather than confine our efforts to our own campus.

Institutes of this type can be incorporated into the partnership once faculty members within their individual disciplines are prepared to assume leadership roles. A similar type of summer institute has been successfully implemented in the field of history by some Pennsylvania liberal arts colleges. The Woodrow Wilson National Fellowship Foundation may be initiating its own history institute in 1989, thus extending its programs in math/science and writing into the humanities. My own interaction with teachers indicates that they would welcome similar programs, in the form of summer institutes and follow-up sessions during the academic year, in literature, philosophy, and art history. They are simply waiting for the partnership to invite them.

Esthetics

In its extensive work concerned with *Academic Preparation for College,* the Education Equality project of the College Board (1983) has identified six major areas that schools and colleges must consider as fundamental: English, the arts, mathematics, science, social studies, and foreign languages. Most educators would agree that these disciplines are fundamental to the educational process, but would also admit that the arts are the most neglected area in the curriculum. Artists in America, Faulkner once said, are nice pets to have around the house. We really do not take the arts as seriously as other cultures do, and they are still marginal to the core disciplines in the curriculum.

Within the past two decades, however, a number of exemplary programs have greatly strengthened the case for arts education. One of the best known is the Esthetic Education Program of the Central Midwestern Educational Laboratories in St. Louis; another is Cleveland's Education for Esthetic Awareness, which concentrates on music; a third is the Kentucky Center for the Arts. These approaches see "the arts in the elementary grades carrying the same weight as social studies, language arts, mathematics, science, and physical education. In other words, the arts are regarded as a sixth major area of study, encompassing art, music, dance, and theatre, with its own general arts program—just as a social studies program might include history, civics, and current events. At the junior and senior high levels, the course of study for the arts involves more discipline-oriented programs" (Madeja and Smith, 1982, p. 1). The image used is that of a tree, with the trunk established in the elementary grades and the branches to the individual disciplines developed when appropriate—usually at the high school level.

One major step toward integrating the arts into the curriculum is to bring teachers in other fields into an esthetic education program that will show how the arts can enhance their work. This can be effectuated most successfully by an educational partnership. One of the finest programs is the Lincoln Center Institute in New York. A natural educational outgrowth of the performance programs at the Lincoln Center for the Performing Arts, the institute promotes "the development of aesthetic education as an important part of learning" and insists that "perceiving and understanding aesthetic qualities in art and in life [are] as basic to enlightened citizenship as understanding the workings of numbers, of words, of man's history and social traditions, and that achieving this very special kind of understanding has an important place in the learning experiences of students, beginning at an early age" (Schubart, 1986, p. 2).

The program itself has a three-step process. The first is a three-week summer session for teachers in the Julliard building at Lincoln Center: "During the session there is active exploration of esthetic concepts which focus upon performed works in dance, drama, and music and museum visits as the texts for study. This process involves:

- engaging in exercises such as developing improvisations, solving a choreographic problem, composing a musical phrase, or using negative and positive space in a visual work
- viewing the work a first time
- identifying esthetic characteristics of the work based on the exercises explored previously
- engaging in additional exercises and discussions designed to explore these characteristics
- examining other works of art in which similar characteristics are present
- viewing the work again and discussing changed perceptions of the work
- designing experiences for students'' (Schubart, 1986, p. 4).

This process is led by teams of institute teaching artists, along with Maxine Greene of Teachers College, Columbia University, who teaches esthetics to the group. The second step involves preparation for the school year, that is, determining which of these works should be made available for performance in the school or at the center. The third step deals with implementation in the classroom.

The Lincoln Center Institute has been extremely successful. Approximately 1,500 teachers from 300 schools in the New York metropolitan area participate, and during the year more than 100,000 students in classes are affected. The model has now been replicated in Rochester, Albany, Syracuse, Binghamton, and Buffalo, New York; Bowling Green, Ohio; Newark, Delaware; Tulsa, Oklahoma; Nashville, Tennessee; San Diego, California, and Houston, Texas. The success of the program is largely due to its clear aims and superb administration. It is a program with an educational purpose and philosophy. As Marc Schubart, its director, has said, "If we develop a larger audience for classical music it is a dividend, but that is not the goal. You don't teach kids to read in order to sell books. They learn to read and then decide what to read. It should be the same in music. We should create musical literacy so that they can make choices" (Maeroff, 1984, pp. C1, C16).

The adaptation of the Lincoln Center program by the

SUNY Purchase Westchester School Partnership illustrates how esthetic education can effectively be integrated into an educational partnership that uses the resources of a college itself. In our situation, we were particularly fortunate, for SUNY Purchase as a college campus had been established in the early 1970s with the explicit intention of developing professional training programs in theater, film, music, dance, and visual arts. Extraordinary faculty and facilities were readily available, and there had been a history of interaction with school districts; in microcosm, we were a Lincoln Center on a college campus. But the model is immediately adaptable to any liberal arts college with programs in theater, art, music, and dance.

The title of the program, "Arts Bridging the Curriculum," signifies its intention: to acquaint teachers of history, the sciences, foreign languages, literature, and other disciplines with a process that can be replicated in the classroom and that will allow them to have their students attend to a work of art in its own esthetic space. Teams of teachers in traditional academic disciplines are selected from ten participating districts—each district has to provide at least three teachers—at the junior-senior high school level. These teams work with teaching artists in their classrooms on units specifically designed by them, using the process learned in the summer institute. This process underscores how a director or actor makes choices in presenting a play and how the interpretation of a drama is reached.

In the discipline of drama, for example, the process focuses on the world of a play. After a planning period from November to July, a three-week summer institute in esthetic education is established at the college campus. The thirty participating teachers work closely with scholars and professionals in drama, concentrating on the production, history, criticism, and esthetics of particular plays. Ideally, these should be plays that are mounted by the college theater program or community theater companies during the academic year so that students can return to see the same plays that the teachers have studied in depth during the summer and then shared with them.

But the important element is the *process:* the production, history, criticism, and esthetics of the chosen play and, most crucially, the ways in which the world of that play can illuminate the study of history, the sciences, foreign languages, and literature. The same type of summer institute can be organized for dance, music, visual arts, and film, and once several are established many interconnections between the arts and the standard disciplines in liberal arts and sciences will inevitably occur. The special structure of an educational partnership—its location on the college campus and its proximity to participating school districts—contributes to the long-range success of an arts program that involves all levels of education because continuity throughout the academic year is feasible. Teaching artists can conduct workshops at the campus that are related to whatever plays may be performed during that academic year, and classroom work in the individual schools can be coordinated with the teaching artists. The teachers and their students can then become an involved audience for all college productions.

The stimulating effect of an esthetics education program on teachers and students is a catalyst for creativity in all disciplines. It opens up new possibilities in the imaginative mode of cognitive learning through performing and visual arts that have their own communications and symbol systems; it involves students and teachers in a process that helps them interpret not only specific art forms but the issues they raise; it offers strategies for expanding students' experiences with literature, social sciences, and other subjects; it renders those works required by any statewide syllabus in language arts more meaningful and more accessible to students.

It is students, of course, who must be the beneficiaries of an esthetics education program. And, with this primary audience in mind, the case cannot be made strongly enough that the arts should occupy a central place in the curriculum because they are and will be a dominant feature in the lives of students, if only as entertainment. Greene, who has been one of the leading advocates of arts education, makes the case cogently and eloquently:

> Our effort is to nurture a crucial, often neglected mode of literacy—what is called esthetic literacy. This involves a deliberate effort to nurture informed

awareness of works of art, a more discriminating appreciation of plays, dance performances, music, paintings, works of literature.

I cannot emphasize enough the importance of this when it comes to moving the young to embark on new beginnings, to choose to learn to learn. It is only when there is a consciousness of something beyond the ordinary, the actual, the taken-for-granted that persons are moved to become different, to use what they have been taught to reach beyond where they are. It seems to me that a school committed to education rather than training is somehow morally obligated to attend to the kinds of values realized here. I have the values of craftsmanship and style in mind among other things. At a moment of carelessness in our society, of a general shoddiness in many places, how many people bring conscience to bear on what they do? How many let their imaginations work and think of what might be, what ought to be, what is not yet? How many are freed to tap the range of their intelligences, of their capacities for being in and attending to the world?

Yes, this is serious. Yes, this is a space for excellence. There are doors to open for those concerned for the growth of persons and for the opening of possibility [1985, pp. 1, 11].

Introducing an esthetics education program into any school district is a formidable task. It requires extraordinary cooperation on the part of the district itself and should have, as Eisner (1987, p. 34) points out, some of the following characteristics:

1. It will have a written curriculum that is employed districtwide in grades K through 12.
2. The content of the art curriculum will have developed from four major disciplines: art production, art criticism, art history, and esthetics.

3. The curriculum is goal oriented, and its activities are sequential in character. What students learn at one point builds upon what has preceded and prepares for what is to come.

4. The art program draws upon resources in the community to enhance what is being provided in the school.

5. Student learning is evaluated so that program strengths and weaknesses can be identified.

6. District policy requires that adequate instructional time be set aside for art instruction and that the visual arts be regarded as a basic part of the students' general education.

7. School administrators and school board members support and encourage discipline-based art education and leave no doubt that instruction in this area is a basic part of the school's program.

8. Finally, this ideal school district will have an evaluation program that determines the extent to which a discipline-based art education curriculum is actually being implemented in the classroom and one that provides useful feedback for teachers for improving curriculum and instruction.

An educational partnership can serve as a catalyst for such an agenda, "the development of multiple forms of literacy" and of "a balanced curriculum." Eisner responds to the fundamental question, "What's in it for our children? . . . . the ability to see, to imagine, to share, and to understand. Not a bad agenda for education" (pp. 34–35).

8

Programs to Strengthen
Career Guidance Counseling

In its final report, *Keeping the Options Open,* prepared for the College Board and published in October 1986, the Commission on Precollege Guidance and Counseling reminds us that "many school reforms have been proposed and enacted in the past few years in the name of achieving excellence in the public schools. While this reform movement has successfully returned public education to the national agenda, it has brought neither increased attention to nor support for guidance and counseling in the schools. In fact, the topic of guidance and counseling has largely been ignored. We think this is an unfortunate omission with serious consequences for children" (Howe, 1986, p. 1).

The need to improve career guidance has been widely recognized for many years and now, with the support of a national commission, will be given even greater attention. Many of the states have already mandated the preparation of guidance plans that include career education. At present, high school students receive little help in learning about their vocational aptitudes, the nature of the work experience, or job opportunities in the area where they live. Some take intensive vocational training, but even those who begin with a narrow perspective may find employment in a field different from the one in which they were trained. Others matriculate in liberal arts colleges, wisely deferring their inevitable career decisions for four years, but at

127

the same time coming to higher education without a sense of those professional opportunities that naturally result from study in the humanities, social sciences, or natural sciences. The remainder leave high school and seek employment in some of the 44,000 different occupations that exist in this country, only partially prepared by the local counseling staff to decide on a career and thus incompletely trained for the world of work. Most of these students, regrettably, are underprivileged youngsters for whom a college education would be extremely useful.

Keeping the Options Open stresses the need to establish "a model of precollege guidance and counseling that is comprehensive and developmental from kindergarten through twelfth grade, and in which guidance counselors are central rather than peripheral to teaching and learning in the schools" (p. 9). It calls for far greater participation of representatives of groups that affect students—"counselors, teachers, administrators, paraprofessionals, students, and parents, with consultation and advice from community service agencies, local colleges, and business" (p. 9)—so that the work of the guidance counselor in the school can be strengthened.

Keeping the Options Open is an important summary of the neglected role of the guidance counselor, a reminder of how central that role should be, and a document that spells out an agenda for action to which decision makers within the schools must respond. It has the authority of the Commission on Precollege Guidance and Counseling, chaired by Harold Howe II, senior lecturer of the Harvard Graduate School of Education and former commissioner of education and composed of other distinguished representatives from universities and colleges, high schools, a foundation, a state employment agency, a state education department, and the National Association of Secondary School Principals. The report is cogent and compelling, but one fears that its recommendations, specific enough but dependent upon the goodwill of school administrators, may be blurred or bypassed by other priorities. There are not strong lobbyists to insist upon implementation of the suggestions—no union or administrative agency—and they may be put aside, as they have so often been in the past. Comprehensive programs such as the two outlined

below are needed to reinforce and implement these sound recommendations. If they can be woven into the fabric of an educational partnership, the full participation advocated by the
commission, which is so essential to the success of any project,
will be achieved.

The need to assert the significance of the guidance counselor is clear. There is a concern on the part of both the college
bound and those who are not going to college to know more about
the expectations and demands of the world of work. Parents and
their children are increasingly concerned with careers, and even
the new reaffirmation of a liberal arts education is largely for
pragmatic reasons. That is, in an age of information, the student with fundamental skills and broad knowledge will have an
even greater chance of success than he or she had in the past.
Students recognize that this is true, but they are confused about
service-related jobs and want to know what skills and knowledge
really are essential for success. Even though we may return to
those traditional skills of written and mathematical literacy as
well as knowledge in the core subjects of the humanities, social
sciences, and natural sciences, a counselor who has held even
a part-time job in the world of work speaks with an authority
that students respect. As the counselor comes to know more
about contemporary employment through his or her personal
involvement in it and is able to share with his or her own students
the experiences of counselors in other schools of the partnership,
recommendations to students will no longer seem academic.

By developing a program specifically for guidance counselors, an educational partnership can dramatically reinforce the
centrality of counseling in the schools. Two highly successful
models have been the Work/Education Fellowship Program of
the Institute for Educational Leadership (IEL), which was implemented in the District of Columbia Public Schools and subur-
ban metropolitan area school systems, and the Fellowship Program for Secondary School Guidance Counselors of the SUNY
Purchase Westchester School Partnership, adapted from the IEL
program.

Both programs have as their centerpiece externships, in
which guidance counselors work during the summer so that their

personal experiences with local businesses and government agencies can help them develop external resource networks and be incorporated into the educational experiences of the students. These are not simply summer externships or short, in-service programs for counselors, but full-year appointments. They respond directly to the recommendations of *Keeping the Options Open* and, beyond their benefits to counselors and students, have the enthusiastic endorsement of employers. Business leaders find that there is efficiency in working with guidance counselors who can reach large numbers of students. With the growth of small businesses, banks, and governmental and hospital agencies, the networking effect for counselors within a partnership is attractive (a counselor in one school can call another for information about a site where the latter worked). Finally, the counselors, with support from their superintendents and principals, provide the one common group upon which employers can depend.

The IEL model is an "eleven-month developmental program structured around three components: (1) informational and training seminars (twice monthly), (2) summer externship with area employers (four weeks), and (3) individual projects (school year)" (Danzberger, 1984, p. 2). The seminars prepare counselors for the summer externships, develop ways in which their work experiences can be used in the school, and help to shape the individual projects. The externships place counselors in jobs that help them see how businesses function, how career paths are structured, and what is expected of new employees; these summer placements "are developed in cooperation with boards of trade, area Chambers of Commerce, Private Industry Councils, and other appropriate organizations of the business community" (Danzberger, 1984, p. 3). The individual projects are directly related to the counselor's work and focus upon "improving career development or employability training in his or her individual school or within the larger system to meet broader system objectives" (p. 3). There is a Fellowship Advisory Committee, composed of representatives from area businesses, local colleges and universities, the IEL, youth service agencies, and administration and teaching staff from the school systems themselves. Arrangements have been made for either academic credit from institutions of higher education or in-service credit from within the school system itself.

The Work/Education Fellowship Program was developed and supported for a two-year demonstration period through a grant from the Ford Foundation and is now an ongoing project of the IEL. The Fellowship Program for Secondary School Guidance Counselors, an adaptation of the SUNY Purchase Westchester School Partnership, concentrates on the networking of guidance counselors throughout twenty-six of the school districts of Westchester County. It too offers information and training seminars before and after the externship, four-week summer employment with local businesses and corporations, and year-long projects that apply the summer externships and seminar experiences to the counselors' schools.

The Purchase program is built upon several assumptions (Mason, 1986, p. 2):

* School counselors themselves . . . have as a rule had few if any opportunities to work in business or industry and may in addition know little about the current opportunities for employment in their own communities.
* Those institutions which normally provide in-service programs for teachers and counselors usually have not developed courses about the changing world of work.
* Counselors are obligated to spend most of their energies steering their students toward colleges and consequently neglect those, still numerous, secondary-level students who badly need advice and preparation for immediate entry into employment.

The special feature of this program is its integral relationship to the college-school collaboration. By having a superintendent chair the committee that prepares the proposal and by having him or her and several other superintendents commit district funds to the project, by having these superintendents urge their colleagues to participate, and by persuading the other superintendents to identify guidance counselors to join the program, the partnership is virtually assured of success. From

the perspective of a college dean, I was able to witness a superintendent and other administrators, several teachers, and numerous guidance counselors respond to a deeply felt but inchoate
need to improve school counseling and work their way toward
a coherent project, largely through the authority of the superintendent in charge of the program. Once again, I was convinced
of the need to have a superintendent lead each project. Despite
the new authority of the union as teachers' benefits are substan-
tially increased, the recent emphasis on "lead" teachers, and
the sensible recommendation (especially in *A Nation Prepared*)
that collaboration among all constituencies is the only pattern
for success, the superintendent still carries enormous authority.
He or she is critical to the success of any project.

At the outset, as I sat at an orientation meeting with
something like thirty guidance counselors to see if the IEL counselor program could be adapted by the Purchase partnership,
I heard nothing but "practical" reasons why it would be very
difficult to achieve this. The funding of the IEL program (an
$800 stipend to each counselor for four weeks of work) was
altogether insufficient for anyone living in Westchester County.
Moreover, the actual function of the guidance counselor at the
work site was very unclear. Was the counselor simply to be a
kind of clerk, an assistant, or would he or she have a real job?
Did we really think that guidance counselors would give up part
of their summers for a program of this kind?

Beyond these pragmatic reservations, the guidance counselors clearly suffered from a lack of status within their schools
and felt as though they were on the periphery of the educational
process. But the presiding superintendent, who had once been
a guidance counselor himself, gave the orientation meeting and
subsequent sessions a positive direction by indicating his own
conviction that the current condition of the guidance counselor
in the schools was an educational scandal, that the counselor
was in fact a pivotal person in the school system, that the IEL
program was the best he had seen in his career of thirty-one
years, and that the financial concerns would be solved through
annual fellowships funded by the school districts and participating businesses. He stressed that this program must be selec-

tive and honorific and that it had to carry an annual stipend adequate to the needs of the counselors—no one should feel exploited or coerced. The figure settled on for each guidance counselor was $2,700. Eight-hundred dollars were needed for administrative costs, so the total budget for one fellow was $3,500.

The funding concerns, which seemed so vexing in the beginning, faded as other superintendents joined their colleagues in committing their school systems to the program. Each participating school district contributed $1,000 and each participating industry paid $2,500, which funded the major portion of the salary for the four-week externship. The funds from the ten participating school districts and industries totaled $35,000 for one school year, and an additional commitment of $10,000 from the ten schools continued the project into the following year, when they had to be implemented in the districts. Each of the counselors received a $2,700 annual stipend, payable in two installments: $2,000 on conclusion of the summer work experience and $700 on completion of the fellowship report at the end of the year.

Once the school districts had agreed to support the project with $2,000 of their own funds, local firms each contributed $2,500. The ten community contributors included Westchester Personnel, the Town of Harrison, CIBA-Geigy (a chemical firm), Kings Electronics, the Bank of New York, the Peoples Westchester Savings Bank, Nestle, IBM, Westchester Medical Center, and Arrowwood (a conference center). In addition, foundation funds allowed us to support a counselor at the Westchester Medical Center to explore careers in the health fields. This list of small local businesses, banks, and community agencies, as well as major corporations, indicates how the guidance counselor program has become a genuine community enterprise.

Before the externships took place, we held a series of seminars, organized by an advisory committee that was led by the president of the Westchester County Association—the equivalent of a Chamber of Commerce. These seminars dealt with the economy of the county, the kind of jobs available, and the future direction of careers. The placements themselves were extremely varied, ranging from work on an assembly line at Kings

Electronics to participation in a bank-teller training program at Bank of New York. The projects that followed the four-week externships signify the meaning of the enterprise. One counselor addressed the needs of grade 12 business students who plan to work after graduation; another took students to individual work sites where they thought they might want to work; a third developed "a banking/preparation" course for students who wanted to qualify as part-time teller trainees, in preparation for possible banking careers; a fourth identified entry-level job opportunities in Westchester County government; a fifth introduced students to positions in civil service through a ten-week freshman advisory program; a sixth created small-group seminars focused on accounting, bookkeeping, marketing, management, computers, engineering, and interviewing; a seventh dealt with eighth graders enrolled in vocational education programs and provided them with a broad view of the labor market as well as the requirements and qualifications necessary to obtain an entry-level job; an eighth worked with middle-school guidance counselors in shaping a career orientation and exploration program; a ninth developed an employment opportunity newsletter for every high school guidance office.

These projects represent the first year's work of the participating guidance counselors and are only formative and suggestive. But the power of suggestion here is considerable and will lead, with the support and validation of a national report such as *Keeping the Options Open,* to the recognition that the guidance counselor is a central figure in the educational process.

Several achievements result from a program of this kind.

In the most direct way—through administrative and financial support of the superintendent—the guidance counselor extends the experience of the externship and the practicality of his or her yearlong project into the fabric of the educational system itself. He or she makes connections with fellow counselors, teachers, administrators, and, most importantly, with the students.

The counselor's efforts are validated not only by school authorities but by the other constituencies of an educational partnership: business, higher education, and the community. By contributing to the support of the counselor, business matches its rhetoric with its funds and with resources at the work site. In the same way, by encouraging a guidance counselor program, higher education indicates that the college-bound student will have a clearer sense of the importance of postsecondary schooling. Finally, when the community understands that this program will benefit all students—those who enter the work force immediately, those who proceed to college, and those who work and then return to college—it will see the mutual reinforcement of education and work. It is difficult to conceive of a more direct way of stating the primacy of education to all students, but especially to underprivileged and unprepared children and their parents for whom the relationship between the long-range effects of education and the immediacy of earning money often seems incongruous.

Within the school districts, the Fellowship Program for Secondary School Guidance Counselors can have an incremental effect of considerable force; and, once again, the educational partnership should become the networking agent. Each project that a guidance counselor develops within his or her particular school is made known to all other counselors in the partnership; each externship opens up a work site for other guidance counselors and their students. Thus a counselor, in the process of guiding a student who wants to know about the conditions within a particular business, can call a colleague who has worked there during his or her fellowship for first-hand information. As the program grows and counselors are placed in different work sites, a reference book should be developed that will list all externships and all counselor projects for the entire educational community. The ultimate effect will be to strengthen not only the guidance counselor but the classroom teacher in making education a reality for students and contributing toward their success—in school and in their ultimate careers.

Any project for guidance counselors depends upon the particular employment opportunities of the local community and will therefore assume its own characteristics. It is critical to assess what the private sector has learned from the experience so that businesses will know how they profit from having counselors at the work site. The project gives them the opportunity to reach into the schools to recruit students for entry-level positions, which are currently difficult to fill. If the project is to have continuity, a communication network must be developed that includes the schools and businesses. An employment opportunity newsletter listing entry-level jobs might be advisable. School counselors should be affiliated with whatever personnel association exists in the area. County businesses might sponsor career days for school districts. These and other ideas will naturally result from the program and contribute toward its institutionalization in the schools, businesses, and community at large.

The Fellowship Program for Counselors illustrates the reinforcing benefits of an educational partnership. Like the programs devoted to motivation and to accelerated and disadvantaged students, teacher-training institutes, and the Center for Leadership Development, this fellowship program is autonomous. With the support of the superintendent and principal, whose strong endorsement is essential, it can function independently. Yet, its deepest and most pervasive success stems from its interaction with those engaged in the other partnership programs. As the collaboration between a college and schools matures, the teachers, administrators, community leaders, students, and guidance counselors will inevitably nourish one another and establish the connections that form the larger pattern of a partnership.

9

Programs for
Leadership Development

In the long run, all partnership programs must culminate in a Center for Leadership Development. Just as the partnership itself is an example of educational leadership, its individual programs are also aspects of the concept. A whole range of administrators is engaged in the many dimensions of leadership, but teachers in their classrooms, guidance counselors in their practice, students in organizations and clubs, community spokespersons, school board members—all these participants in a partnership can profit from a leadership center. Such a center must reach into the entire community, for it needs full participation and involvement if it is to succeed. A Center for Leadership Development illustrates one of the basic themes of this book: educational problems can only be solved through the support and interaction of the total community.

A Center for Leadership Development should be the flagship program in a college-school partnership and integrate its different units, solidify its structure, and become the creative nexus for other activities. Three kinds of programs naturally suggest themselves as the most feasible administrative organization for such a center:

- workshops for administrators, teachers, and students
- a liberal arts curriculum that investigates and illuminates the impact of leadership on past and present cultures

- a wide range of public programs that connect the colleges and schools to their communities

For the most part, these units have functioned separately in colleges and universities, and they have often been successful. Except in one or two instances, however, they have not yet been brought together to form the larger structure of a Center for Leadership Development, and they have not begun to extend the center or any of its units through the powerful delivery system of an educational partnership.

The need for coherence is clear, and programs in educational leadership have been developed at Duke University, Colorado College, and elsewhere to provide it. Still, the deeper connection between the liberal arts curriculum and students' preparation for a significant role in society has not been made, nor has the bridge been built between the university and its several audiences to effect, in Robert Bellah's terms, a "public dialogue" that will "provide moral leadership" (Desruisseaux, 1986, p. 19). One comprehensive way of developing workshops of value to administrators and teachers, a curriculum that will engage students, and service activities for community leaders is through a college-school partnership, which can connect the educational system with government, business, labor, social agencies, and other institutions.

Leadership in American society can no longer be relegated to a few people who through their exceptional, charismatic qualities define directions for the rest of us, their followers. Leadership must occur at every level of society, and it depends ultimately upon what Gardner has called "networks of responsibility": "The first duty of our dispersed leaders is to establish communication among the highly organized (and often warring) segments of our society—business, labor, farmers, professional groups, and so on—to reweave the social fabric. . . . We must develop networks of leaders who accept some measure of responsibility for the society's shared concern. Call them *networks of responsibility,* leaders of disparate or conflicting interests who undertake to act together in behalf of the shared concerns of the community or nation" (1986, p. 102). Gardner's egalitarian definition of leadership is particularly useful for our purposes: "Leadership is the process of persuasion and example by which an individual (or leadership team) induces a group to take action in accord with the leader's purposes or the shared purposes of all" (p. 6). The development of "networks of responsibility" gives sharp focus to how useful collaboration between a college and schools can be, for the collaboration can succeed only if responsibility is taken by all its participants.

Workshops

The most coherent leadership training thus far developed has taken the form of workshops offered to administrators and those considering administrative careers. They are largely drawn from the experiences of management training divisions in corporations and rest on the assumption that both educators and corporate managers confront essentially the same issues. In addition to the growing number of books and articles concerned with management and leadership, there is now a cottage industry producing mountains of materials for leadership programs. These exercises tend to draw upon the work of managerial experts such as Hersey and Blanchard (1982), Peters and Waterman (1985), and Bennis and Namus (1985) as well as upon films such as *Twelve O'Clock High* and video clips on creativity and the delegation of authority. These materials are used for sessions devoted to situational leadership, understanding people, creative problem solving, improved communications, uses of power and authority, time management, and team building.

Three of the most successful programs initiated during the past ten years are the Harvard Institute for Educational Management, the IBM Education Executive Program, and the University of Maryland's Leadership Development Program. They are worth describing in some detail.

The Harvard Institute for Educational Management, which was founded in 1970, offers perhaps the most impressive educational program for the training and retraining of senior-level educational administrators in higher education. A four-week summer program led by an eclectic faculty "chosen specifically for their blend of practical experience in the field and their teaching ability,'' the institute accommodates approximately ninety participants each summer. Those attending are senior administrators sponsored by their own institutions. The institute is expensive—$6,000 for four weeks—and selective; administrators must be nominated by their colleges or universities. The subjects range from ''monitoring the environment'' and ''setting directions'' to ''marshaling resources and support'' and ''managing implementation.'' At the 1986 institute, specific topics included leadership, marketing, law and higher education, introduction to personal computers and wordprocessing, labor relations, strategic planning, assessment and excellence in higher education, managing stress, financial management and control, the political process, and status of minorities. The subjects covered go far beyond management training and are worth replicating.

The IBM Education Executive Program was specifically established to serve educational administrators. It drew upon the corporation's management training program, and its instructors were all IBM trainers. IBM supported the program for twelve months with a subsidy of more than $1 million and ran a continuing weekly program. Each Sunday evening a group of twenty-four administrators convened to begin the following five-day, intensive program:

Sunday	Computer training management
Monday	Introductions
	Managing for achievement
	Situational leadership
	Computer-enhanced management
Tuesday	Creative problem solving
	The Merchantville case
Wednesday	One-to-one people management
	Communications network
	Computer-enhanced management

Thursday	Understanding people
	Ninety-day plan
	Managing management time
Friday	Productivity and team effort

Administrators were encouraged to come in teams so that a superintendent, assistant superintendent, and principal would typically attend from a given school district. The ninety-day plan encouraged administrators to take the techniques learned in the previous five days and develop a specific program in the home school district to which they were returning.

The premise of the Education Executive Program was that management concepts and techniques are as applicable to school administrators as they are to managers in industry. Of course, these concepts and techniques are transferable only if school organizations support a culture based on IBM's basic beliefs—"respect for the individual, service to the customer, and excellence as a way of life"—and its leading principles—managers must lead effectively, there are obligations to the stockholders, there must be fair dealings with suppliers, and IBM must be a good corporate citizen. These beliefs and principles, leaders of the program argued, are fundamental to good leadership anywhere; they simply need to be translated into an academic setting.

For each of the exercises during the week, excerpts from the current literature served as background. Included were selections from essays, reprints from books, and handouts dealing with "The Motivation to Work"; "Stress"; "Downsizing—How to Manage More with Less"; "Situational Leadership" by Paul Hersey and Ken Blanchard; "Creative Meetings Through Power Sharing" by George M. Prince; "Planning on the Left Side and Managing on the Right" by Henry Mintzberg, as well as a personal analysis—"Leader Effectiveness and Adaptability Description (LEAD)"—that allows a participant to recognize and modify, if necessary, his or her own leadership style. Also presented were case histories of difficult problems confronted by school districts. These histories are particularly valuable, for they reveal how essential all participants in a school system, from the school board member to the individual teacher, are to the resolution of conflicts.

The IBM Education Executive Program accomplished its goals; it distilled the essence of the corporation's most effective approaches to management and leadership and persuaded administrators to adapt them to their own school settings. By bringing together teams of administrators from different parts of the country and integrating them with others in groups of twenty-four, the program was able to reinforce application of these approaches in local districts and, at the same time, avoid parochialism. One felt the absence of a school administrator as an instructor since so many of the exercises and so much of the conversation inevitably turned upon specific educational problems. Nevertheless, as a corporate training program and a service to educators, the Education Executive Program was exemplary. The testimonials of gratitude from the more than 1,300 participants validated the program, and there were undoubtedly some applications and follow-through in local districts. The IBM leaders were keenly aware that the program needed to be continued in the school districts themselves, and they developed workshops for those participants who wished to return for training as teachers. Some ninety became trainers and had varying success in extending the IBM Education Executive Program into their own districts; more than seven-eighths in the "train-the-trainer follow-up" felt that they were well prepared to be instructors in the subject matter. But once the corporation ceased to support the project financially, it became impossible to have any genuine continuation of it. Like so many excellent programs of its kind, the Education Executive Program was never fully institutionalized and therefore remains only an example, if not an historical artifact, of what can be done when a first-rate corporation, with its rich resources, works with educational leaders.

A leadership development program of another kind has been conducted at the University of Maryland since 1947. The Creative Leadership Program is primarily for corporate, governmental, and military leaders, and it concentrates on the legitimate uses of power and authority. Its definition of leadership is instructive: "Leadership in the organizational setting is the *process* of recognizing and effectively utilizing legitimate structural and/or situational *power* to *influence* others toward the accomplishment of organizational objectives'' (Lathrop, 1985, p. 16). Power comes from the control of these resources, which then allow for reward and punishment. Jimmy Breslin's definition, quoted in the material, is probably as good as any: ''Power is relative. If you think you've got it, you've got it. If you don't think you have it, even if you have it you don't have it'' (p. 16). And Bennis' remarks give added point to this growing interest in power: ''Power is the last of the little dirty secrets. People who have it don't want to talk about it; people who don't have it don't want to talk about it'' (Bennis, 1974, p. 62). The University of Maryland program underscores the need to understand the nature of power and authority before effective leadership can occur. It draws upon the work of John P. Kotter of the Harvard Business School, who has concerned himself with ''power, dependence, and effective management'' (1977, p. 127), Walter P. Nord (''Developments in the Study of Power,'' 1984), and David C. McClelland and David H. Burnham (''Power Is the Great Motivator,'' 1976). The case method is again an important part of the program and of the exercises.

The IBM Education Executive Program and the University of Maryland's Creative Leadership Program represent two types of leadership development programs. Others are now appearing across the country: the leadership programs at Charlotte/Mecklenburg, Virginia, and at SUNY Purchase are offsprings of the Education Executive Program; the Center for Studies in Creativity at SUNY Buffalo has grown dramatically since it began in 1976; Harvard University sponsors a Principal's Institute and programs for superintendents, which now are replicated elsewhere in the country. Finally, the Department of Education has initiated a ''$7.17 million program designed to help elementary and secondary school administrators improve their leadership skills'' (*Federal Register*, 1986, p. 33218); the program grows out of ''Leadership Administration Development programs . . . authorized in 1984'' (p. 33218). It is clear, as the authors of ''The 'Myth' of the Great Principal'' indicate, that it is impractical to expect someone to provide both ''school management and instructional leadership'' (Rallis and Highsmith, 1987, p. 18). These ''two separate tasks . . . cannot be

performed by a single individual'' and schools need to ''rethink
their leadership structure'' (p. 18). One solution to this dilemma
is to have the leaders of the Center for Leadership Development
work with the principal on the managerial concerns of the school,
thus releasing him or her to be an instructional leader.

Workshops provide an invaluable network for all partnership programs since they will ultimately include the entire
educational community. Furthermore, the Center for Leadership Development itself provides exposure to the political aspect
of leadership. Simply by being a laboratory for leadership, it
allows people to form networks and becomes a living opportunity for leadership development. McCall has underscored this
point: ''Political activity in the sense of developing and maintaining a network of contacts throughout the organization and
its environment is a real part of managerial work. Research has
not revealed much about how these networks are created and
utilized, but most people in leadership roles know how important contacts can be. Many of the contacts are in nonauthority
relationships with the leader, and this may be the arena where
the critical social and political influence aspects of leadership
are played out. Certainly, leadership research and theory should
begin including this dimension, and practitioners might look
at some of their problems in 'getting things done' in light of
their own interconnectedness with key people in the organization'' (1977, p. 16).

The initial audience for the workshops will almost certainly be administrators at all levels of education, and this is
really as far as the programs mentioned above have gone. But
it is important, if one wishes to institutionalize these workshops
into the partnership and the real life of the college or university,
to integrate representatives from other constituencies as well:
school board members; business executives and managers; secre-
taries and staff members; teachers, who after all are ''administrators'' in the classrooms and role models for their students;
government and community leaders; and student leaders of different clubs and organizations. The composition of the workshops should be a microcosm, not only of the partnership but
of society itself.

By involving all participants of the partnership, the Center for Leadership Development can go beyond traditional programs largely devoted to training administrators and create its own, sharper focus: the development of leaders within both the public schools and colleges and universities that would make partnerships between schools and colleges possible. The need is very great indeed at both levels of education. Leadership within the public schools has deliberately and inadvertently been taken away from teachers themselves and lodged with administration. Although superintendents and principals can and should profit from the workshops of a Center for Leadership Development, they must develop leadership from teachers as well if the center and its programs are to succeed over time. Within colleges and universities, administrative leadership faces an almost opposite condition: the autonomy of faculty and a largely untrained and poorly functioning set of middle-level administrators. Bringing together representatives from these different constituencies will not only encourage the concept of partnership but will fructify it, sustain it, and establish the dispersal of accountable leadership throughout the different programs—those "networks of responsibility" that Gardner has called for. Thus teachers, faculty, and middle-level administrators as well as superintendents, presidents, vice presidents, and deans can participate. Eble (1978) has a useful account of the need to improve the quality of academic administrators in *The Art of Administration,* and the American Council in Education has been actively stressing the development of leadership in these middle-level administrators.

Leaders of the workshops need to be as varied as the participants. A corporate trainer, either on loan or permanently in residence, should be part of the team, joined by a school officer, a superintendent or principal, a college administrator, several school and college faculty, and leaders from student affairs. The workshops, as one unit in a Center for Leadership Development, can become a centerpiece to the partnership itself and a gathering place for its various constituents. It can attract educational, corporate, governmental, and human service administrators, who have been driven in their own careers to become leaders and to understand the dimensions of leadership. Most importantly, the workshops can invite faculty and students who are rarely considered in the development of leadership roles. If we want "lead teachers," as *A Nation Prepared* advocates, and more "involvement in learning," no better fulcrum can be created than a Center for Leadership Development within a college-school collaboration. In time, as the workshops become established, the leaders can serve as consultants to school districts and other agencies that may need advice on specific managerial questions or may want them to offer special sessions that contribute to team building.

Curriculum

Workshops and specialized programs, however superb they may be, do not institutionalize the concept of leadership. At best, they create a sense of authentic educational partnership throughout the schools and colleges and their diverse publics; at worst, they are an ephemeral experience. In a college or university, the curriculum is the coin of the realm, and until some academic program gives coherence to the meaning and dimensions of leadership, it will remain marginal to the main interest of the campus.

The most comprehensive survey of leadership programs and courses in higher education is *Leadership Education: A Source Book* (1987), edited by Freeman, Gregory, and Clark and published by the Center for Creative Leadership in Greensboro, North Carolina. It reveals that most initial efforts have been primarily devoted to single courses in the curriculum, although professional and excurricular programs have begun to take shape, and some colleges and universities are attempting to mount comprehensive majors in leadership education.

Some examples of individual courses will suggest the direction now being taken in leadership studies. At the College of Wooster in Massachusetts, James A. Hodges offers "Leadership: Theory and Practice," which concerns itself with definitions of leadership, the various styles leadership assumes, and the ways in which people finally do lead. At Louisiana State

University, a seminar entitled "The Dimensions and Dilemmas of Leadership" centers "on the theme that leadership is an art form whose effectiveness is improved by the mastery of leadership research and by the display of personal integrity—that effective leadership builds on both technical and ethical foundations." At Trenton State College, the Human Relations Department offers a course entitled "Dynamics of Leadership" that deals with leadership theory, organizational development and goal setting, motivation, conflict resolution, and the creative process.

Leadership courses are most often located within professional programs. The Department of Nursing and Health Care Management at the Metropolitan State College in Denver has designed a course "to foster the development of leadership roles of the nurse in working with individuals, families, groups, and communities striving for high-level wellness," and it concentrates on "the nurse as a change agent." At Stanford University, a course called "Issues in Leadership" uses twentieth-century literature . . . to examine some central issues of organizational leadership," and works as varied as Chinua Achebe's *Things Fall Apart,* Eugene O'Neill's *The Iceman Cometh,* Yasumari Kawabata's *The Sound of the Mountain,* and Susan Sontag's *Under the Sign of Saturn* serve as illustrations. Ronald Heifetz at Harvard's John F. Kennedy School of Government deals with "Leadership and the Mobilization of Group Resources." Topics include leadership and the process of educating groups, leadership and the nature of work, leadership and creativity, and leadership and authority.

Women's Studies programs have naturally taken great interest in this field. One example is "Leadership Education for Women," a course offered at SUNY Oswego, with emphasis on "theoretical and practical instruction in leadership, motivation, and organizational development." Another is the "Women's Leadership Program" at Mount St. Mary's in Los Angeles, which began eleven years ago as a seminar for fifteen students with the college president and is now a core multidisciplinary curriculum open to all students, with primary emphasis on community education. Finally, student organizations have begun

to stress formal programs; the College of Lake County, Grays-
lake, Illinois, has designed a course called "College Organization and Government," which is "designed for a select group
of students involved in college organizations, leadership positions, and is open to student officers in college clubs and organizations, members of the student senate, and students serving
on college committees."

It is natural that professional programs, women's studies,
and student organizations should find a significant place for
leadership development. Some colleges and universities have
taken the first steps toward the more ambitious effort of establishing whole programs. At Lebanon Valley College in Pennsylvania, the course of study is called "The Leadership Imperative." It is a "four-level program designed to help promising high school students, collegians, middle managers, and top
executives become more creative and productive leaders." The
college program includes a wide range of courses, from leadership studies to communications, organizational leadership, ethics,
and values. Duke University now has the Leadership Program,
established with a $1 million gift and located in the Institute
of Policy Sciences and Public Affairs. The introductory course,
called "Leadership, Policy, and Change," focuses on "the lives
and experiences of significant leaders, better ones and worse."
Collateral work is then offered in political science, the ROTC
program, public speaking, history, and psychology. A second
unit involves students in "leadership projects," and a third has
internships for "students to work with decision makers who are
intensely involved in some of the more intractable problems of
our society and world."

The last all-college program worth mentioning, and the
most ambitious and impressive one, is led by Thomas Cronin
at Colorado College. A basic course, "Leadership 2000," provides the foundation for the program and includes all elements
of the campus: "[This all-college program] involves student,
faculty, and staff in the study of leadership and the training of
leaders. 'Leadership 2000' supports workshops, public forums,
block-break symposia, and other activities involved in leadership training. In addition, it provides interested students with

lists of courses on leadership, courses which range from 'The American Presidency,' 'Hitler and Stalin,' to 'Urban Politics,' and 'The Hero and Anti-Hero in Literature.' 'Leadership 2000' also maintains a film and videocassette library dealing with leadership, and works with the Student Life Staff and Outward Bound office on campus to coordinate leadership training sessions" (Freeman, Gregory, and Clark, 1987, p. 200).

The Colorado College program reaches far beyond the curriculum to include the residence hall program, leisure activities, college committees, student organizations, and the career center in an attempt to create a holistic approach for students. It has a summer institute devoted to "leadership and governance in America" that synthesizes the program through readings, films, and guest lectures. It also has a special focus in its newly established McHugh Chair of American Institutions and Leadership, currently occupied by Cronin.

The curriculum gives intellectual substance to what might otherwise be construed as merely practicums. While the curriculum will be only as compelling as those who create it, certain elements recur so often that they must be considered seriously in any academic program devoted to leadership:

- a foundation course devoted to leadership theory and practice
- individual courses in philosophy, history, political science, psychology, literature, and sociology
- courses for student leaders, offered through the division of student affairs
- courses concerned with college organization and governance, offered by the administration
- an individualized senior project that personalizes the student's learning and causes him or her to write significantly and at length on an aspect of leadership
- an internship that places the student with a decision maker and highlights the significance of citizenship and community service

There is more, much more, and the programs are growing so rapidly that no description or catalogue can contain them;

but the six elements I have noted run through all these courses and programs concerned with leadership education and are clearly essential. I would hesitate to recommend a formal major in the undergraduate curriculum, for there is the danger of professionalizing the field, isolating it in either a department of the liberal arts college or in a separate school, institute, or center and making it less central to the entire curriculum. Leadership studies do not represent a discipline like philosophy, sociology, or chemistry; they are inherently multidisciplinary and reflective of broad human concerns, and the individual courses probably should be clustered in a minor, concentration, or program.

Public Service

Public service is organic to the very concept of a partnership between a college and schools. A Center for Leadership Development will naturally invite well-known speakers to give lectures or conduct seminars on special topics and will ask the community to participate when appropriate. By making public service activities a formal part of the center and by establishing it as a major unit of the college-school collaboration, partnership leaders will relate those activities to the workshops, the curriculum, and by extension to all aspects of the partnership itself.

The effectiveness of this dimension of leadership education is demonstrated by the Aspen Institute for the Humanities in Aspen, Colorado. The institute conducts extended seminars for business executives and managers on a broad range of liberal arts subjects, from Renaissance art to contemporary literature. The seminars, conducted by college faculty, are supported by firms and are viewed as ways to stimulate, broaden, and enrich the lives of their personnel. It should prove no more difficult to conduct such seminars as part of the ongoing activities of the Center for Leadership Development.

At Purchase, we have begun to associate several public programs with our ongoing workshops and curriculum development. In the 1988–89 academic year, for example, two events will illustrate how a partnership can embrace the larger community. The first is a daylong conference in the fall that will be built around the responsibility of school boards, using the highly successful publication of the IEL, *School Boards,* as the basis for discussion with Michael Usdan and other authors. The spring conference will be concerned with networking and use the accumulated experience and wisdom of Seymour Sarason, Saul Cohen, Elizabeth Lorentz, and others who have published extensively on the subject. These conferences will be invitational to the appropriate audiences, and they will be followed up by meetings specifically directed toward institutionalizing the recommendations made by leaders and participants. In every program and teaching institute of our partnership, follow-up is mandated so that the event itself is not extrinsic to the operation of the partnership districts. These public meetings can become important forums for community leadership on educational matters.

There is no definitive structure for a leadership program within an educational partnership, but practical workshops, a clearly presented curriculum, and public service activities seem to suggest themselves naturally. Cohering them into a Center for Leadership Development and having that center devoted to reinforcing all of the programs in the college-school collaboration by having their participants attend the leadership workshops gives the partnership a focus that can in turn lend direction to all activities.

This will not be a simple or easy task. A major reason for the absence of leadership is that major social institutions—the family, church, and community as well as the school and university—have lost their authority; and it is against this atomization of American society that leadership training must be encouraged. Goodlad underscores the difficulties in shaping a coherent program in leadership:

> Not only have the coalitions that created and sustained the education system withered, but the institutions comprising a significant part of these coalitions have weakened significantly. The family rivals the school in the loss of stability. Home, school, and religious institutions no longer join as

they once did in rearing the young. Further, a
secondary school that once enrolled only a fraction
of the age group—and those young people most
supported by other institutions in the coalition—
has become part of the common school. The problems of dealing with student diversity grow ever
greater. Perhaps most serious of all, the parental
and solid-citizen role models of an intimate community and the heroes of virtue of earlier times have
been largely replaced by the glamorized lives of
"beautiful people" and athletes whose exploits are
made exotic and larger than life by attentive media.
The role of education in enculturation is threatened
by serious imperfections in the culture itself [1986,
pp. 3–4].

One proceeds therefore with cautious optimism—with
what Emerson called pragmatic idealism. On the global scale,
Burns is certainly justified in saying that "one of the most universal cravings of our time is a hunger for compelling and creative
leadership. . . . The crisis of leadership today is the mediocrity
or irresponsibility of so many men and women in power"
(Burns, 1978, p. 7). And for those of us in schools, colleges,
businesses, and governmental agencies who seek to build an
educational partnership and create something like a coherent
program of leadership studies within that partnership, Burns's
further statements must be disturbing: "We know far too little
about *leadership*. . . . Leadership is one of the most observed and
least understood phenomena on earth. . . . There is, in short,
no school of leadership, intellectual or practical" (p. 7).

A partnership can begin to create that school of leadership by first anchoring it in the liberal arts themselves and then
extending it outward, through the college-school collaboration,
to schools, businesses, community agencies, and government
agencies. It can involve representatives from these different
groups in workshops on leadership that create "networks of
responsibility" throughout the region that the partnership serves.
And it can formulate a curriculum that stresses the significance

of leadership studies. Such studies should not be in a separate professional program, or in an institute at the edge of the liberal arts college, or in isolated workshops and courses. Like the college-school collaboration itself, leadership studies should find their home in the college of liberal arts and sciences, which is the center of the college or university. Workshops, curriculum, and public events must be brought together creatively so that the partnership can begin the difficult process of creating what Bellah has called "an education for the training of leadership and public service in a free society" (Desruisseaux, 1986, p. 19).

10

❦❦❦❦❦❦

Ensuring the Long-Term Success of College-School Partnerships

We no longer have to make the case for the concept of college, school, and business collaborations. They are a reality in virtually every community. The directory that the American Association for Higher Education has recently published, with more than 1,000 collaborative enterprises catalogued, indicates the power of the movement. Many of these efforts are modest: adopt-a-school programs between businesses and schools, college courses for high school students, corporate funding of special programs. But others are much more ambitious. The Advanced Placement Program, Project Advance, the National Faculty, the Academic Alliances, the National Network for Educational Renewal, and the other partnerships described in Chapter One have gone far beyond the experimental stage and are reforming the landscape of learning in America.

It is not the idea of partnership that needs ratification but its goals and aims, its structure and strategy, its future direction. As with many new movements, individual enterprises have emerged and have had varying success. Certain programs—for gifted and at-risk students, for teachers in the disciplines, for administrators who seek guidance in leadership—have been featured in most partnerships, and organizational strategies are as various as the collaborations themselves. Each educational partnership will find its own form as a result of its own needs, but the pattern that I have recommended would seem applicable

154

to most colleges, schools, businesses, and governmental agencies within the same community. I want now to make the most forceful argument I can for its replication and adaptation throughout state colleges and universities and the schools nearest them.

The following recommendations are fundamental to the long-range success of an educational partnership:

1. *The donor* must provide significant funding over a three-to-five-year period to launch the enterprise. A partnership that involves a college and ten school districts with a total of 20,000 to 30,000 students will require at least $200,000 as catalyst support.

2. *The college* should be the administrative home of the partnership and contribute office space and other facilities for events and activities.

- *Annual dues* must be paid by participating districts, once the partnership has established itself, to replace the original grant. These dues as well as support from the college should provide core support—for the staff and its facilities—so that institutionalization is effected.
- *Fiscal autonomy* should be sought for all projects, although some may need start-up monies from the core funding.

3. *The dean of liberal arts and science* ought to be the chairperson of the partnership unless his or her counterpart in a strong education program is eager to assume leadership and work with the liberal arts disciplines.

- *Superintendents* must form the steering or policy committee, agree to serve as leaders of individual projects, and represent their districts at all meetings of the steering committee.
- *An executive director,* full time and from the school culture, needs to be hired and given as much core staff support as the budget will allow.
- *Project directors* should be chosen from both the college and school cultures and be given as much autonomy as possible.
- *The executive director and his or her immediate staff* should become part of the college budget as the initial external funding

expires, thus allowing the annual dues of districts to provide
for the growth of programs.

- *Teachers* must be actively involved in advisory committees
for all projects.
- *A process evaluator* should be engaged at the outset to work
with all the above participants, but especially with the dean
and executive director.

4. *Realistic expectations* seem particularly important, a sense
of *proportion* critical. An educational partnership may want to
become a microcosm of all that is needed in American education, but it must maintain a proper relationship to other college and school activities if it is to survive and maintain quality
growth.

These recommendations are incremental and merely formative. Their further development will include research and
development, assessment of programmatic impact on the students themselves, and the possibility of replication throughout
state universities and other consortia of colleges. An educational
partnership is finally a process, not a product, and is limited
only by the imagination, talent, and energy of its participants.

The first few years of a partnership are so demanding that
the dean, a few superintendents, and the executive director must
be willing to lend time well beyond that devoted to the jobs for
which they are formally held accountable. As a dean, I was fortunate to find colleagues who were there when I needed them
most. We have built bridges that now connect the schools and
the college, local businesses, corporations, and governmental
agencies. These bridges have converged at the college itself,
which is the nexus of the partnership, and have created a new
kind of educational system. The bridges are strongest where they
converge—stronger than any single unit and linked by cooperation rather than by competition. Before, there were disparate
efforts, marginal activities, mere aspirations. Now there is a permanent educational partnership. The same can happen, I am
convinced, in the 3,200 liberal arts units of community colleges,
four-year colleges, and universities in the country. Such a movement will go far toward creating a mutual estate in American
education.

Ours is a culture of separation and American education is a reflection of that culture. If the sixties and seventies suffered from moral and intellectual relativism, we have since been searching for connections that will create a true educational system, a meaningful tradition, and a sense of order and community. We need to forge a collaboration between the different levels of schooling and between education and its diverse publics. Partnerships are one pragmatic response to the atomization that is corroding American education and society.

The concept of collaboration has taken root and will grow because the benefits to colleges, schools, businesses, communities, and government are so palpable and far-reaching. Partnerships begin in self-interest, grow as a result of shared values, and culminate in service to all their participants.

Service to the public is an important responsibility of state colleges and universities, and a partnership satisfies that requirement directly. From a self-interested perspective, collaboration with the schools is the best possible recruitment method for colleges. Through student programs, teaching institutes, and a Center for Leadership Development, the partnership brings to campus educators and community representatives who meet college faculty and project leaders, work in their laboratories and other facilities, interact with administrators informally, and then return to their own students with an intimate knowledge of the college. High school students who come to a college's campus can measure the quality of its faculty, and faculty and teachers in the same disciplines can work with one another. Although the concept of partnership may not be initially welcome to all faculty, especially to those committed to research, they will inevitably see its benefits to recruitment.

As the partnership develops, some faculty will become increasingly aware of the needs of local schools, and they will work to develop joint academic programs. Others may agree to teach in those programs for extra compensation, while still others will become directors of projects. Some may begin to see the enormous research potentialities of a partnership and develop grant proposals, which will now have an applied character to them and may well prove to be extremely successful because they enjoy the broad support of school administrators, faculty, students, and their communities. Within each proposal will be requests for supplies and equipment that remain at the college long after the grant has expired. For example, the Natural Sciences Division at Purchase was able to retain the twelve persona' computers that were part of three proposals for a teachers institute in the sciences funded by IBM. Although they are at the service of the institute during the summer, they are used by the science faculty during the academic year.

The most obvious benefit of a partnership to schools is economic. Although Goodlad and others have made a convincing case that a small school is usually better, at a certain point reduced size means severely limited services—fewer advanced placement courses, for instance, and less specialized work for the children of demanding parents. The participation of the college or university lends prestige to the collaboration and focuses attention on the disciplines themselves. The teacher who is intellectually lonely—so often there is only one chemistry teacher in a small high school—finds colleagues from other schools with whom he or she can share concerns, and the partnership helps to turn a "job" into a "profession." Then there is the flexibility that the college-school collaboration provides: workshops, seminars, and summer programs can be initiated far more rapidly than they can be organized in the schools.

In a direct sense, the partnership allows the concerns of the classroom to be directed by the teachers themselves. The teachers help to shape the subject of the teachers institutes and inevitably go far beyond the action plan of a state's education department. In New York there was a wave of discontent when the state action plan of the New York state regents dictated requirements that teachers thought were unrealistic. Moreover, although there were many statewide forums at which they could voice their objections, they also resisted what they felt was a paternalistic way of setting educational standards and goals. A partnership allows teachers to own the programs they have helped to create.

There need not be a polarization between a state's department of education and the partnership in terms of aims. In the process of developing our economics and foreign language institutes, for example, we have been keenly aware of state guidelines that require all students to have minimum knowledge of the subjects. It would be foolish and self-defeating not to comply with these guidelines. Indeed, the rapid success of our institutes has been largely due to pressure from the state action plan. Finally, the school superintendents, school board members, and teachers can broaden their perspective through the partnership and avoid a sense of isolation and parochialism. Even the wealthiest district cannot mount the spectrum of programs that I have described. They need the college or university to match pedagogy with research, and they require a reasonably sophisticated development office, present in virtually every college, to help raise funds in the private sector.

Without the schools, there can be no partnership; without the partnership, the schools are more limited and potentially more parochial, less flexible, less close to the genuine interests of all participants. It is an ideal marriage in that a school system can take what it needs from the partnership. In practice, the projects are appealing to almost all the districts because the superintendents approved of them initially, with at least three agreeing to furnish support.

The structure of the college-school collaboration gives the superintendents control over program development so that very little remains theoretical, even though college faculty will be bringing a wealth of scholarship and research to each effort. There is thus a direct match between the needs of the schools and the programs implemented by the partnership. In this sense, the partnership is viewed as a resource and a supplement to instruction, inviting experimentation but also implementing programs that no single school district could afford alone. As these pieces of the partnership are put together, attention to coherent design must be the responsibility of the dean and the executive director, working closely with the steering committee. The partnership may grow, as ours has from eleven to twenty-six school districts and two BOCES, but the dean will eventually find him- or herself sorting out priorities, setting the agenda, planning the future with the executive director, and taking recommendations to the steering committee for consideration. Programmatic coherence must come from these two leaders, working closely together.

The greatest problem with the schools is maintaining their interest in the partnership. Colleges and schools have an economic hold on their employees, but the partnership has none. As soon as it falters or a district has problems of its own, the danger of withdrawal becomes immediate. The partnership is viewed as a marginal activity, especially in the beginning and even after it has achieved some success, and it will become the first program to be sacrificed by a school board if cutbacks become necessary. The sign of success will be when districts see the partnership as indispensable to their interests. In this sense, a partnership between a college and schools is always a delicate organism. The only ways that one can assure continuing growth are by involving the superintendents in the supervision of individual programs that will enhance their prestige with their school boards and by making districts pay not only dues to the partnership but funds for each of the projects. Two of the educational clichés of the moment are empowerment and ownership, but both of these are in fact essential for superintendents, principals, and teachers. A partnership is a cornucopia of educational activities for them and offers them every opportunity to take leadership of individual projects.

A corporation profits from the partnership in terms of public service and image. It is paying its civic dues, but it is also—and this point needs to be stressed whenever one approaches business for funds—investing in its own future and collaborating with the schools in what is really a joint venture. The benefits to business are very direct. Children of employees attend schools within partnership districts; businesses will not need to provide some of their current training programs in basic skills if new workers are properly educated; and the better the quality of the school districts, the easier time businesses and corporations will have in attracting new employees from elsewhere.

I need not elaborate upon the need that schools and colleges have for private support. Collaboration is a mutual investment in the future of the country. As William Woodside has argued, taxes must provide sufficient support. No amount of private support should blur the primary obligation of the public sector. Business serves as a catalyst, helping to initiate programs, but it must inevitably withdraw once the program is successfully launched and then go on to another program, another frontier.

The danger in corporate involvement is the tendency of corporate or foundation officers to make gratuitous suggestions, to reorder priorities, or to insist upon satisfaction of their own agendas. The relationship between educational institutions and corporations is always precarious. Once the gift has been made, however, with whatever conditions the schools and colleges accept, business must keep a distance and ask simply for an evaluation of the project.

The community enjoys the presence of a partnership that improves its schools and to which it can contribute in a variety of advisory roles. Parents see immediately that programs their schools could individually never afford now become possible.

I am sure that there are dangers in community involvement, and one reads periodically of groups everywhere in the country exerting pressure that can only complicate the educational process. We did not experience these problems, partially because we were at a remove from the taxpayers and school boards, but basically for two reasons that will apply to any collaboration between a college and schools. The programs of the partnership, so carefully screened by superintendents who were sensitive to the reactions of parents, were always an enhancement of community efforts and therefore were viewed positively. We were, after all, in a constant process of augmenting the tax dollars of the districts with funding from the private sector or the State Education Department or federal agencies. Second, we listened hard to our corporate donors, the parents, and community leaders; we assimilated their best ideas into our proposals; and we altered them to fit guidelines. Moreover, we obviously stretched as far as we could for support, without compromising the fundamental principles of any given proposal. But after all these efforts, we made a distinction between advice and accountability. After we received the advice from all these other constituencies, we as educators—leaders of the schools and college who composed the steering committee—made the decisions.

162 Partners in Education

Government benefits from partnerships by having other sectors of the society, especially business, share in the responsibility of education. Cohen has made the argument well:

> Today's widespread concern over the plight and future of our public schools is unparalleled, and rightfully so. We've been down the path of national concern for school reform before—but with limited success. The focus on science and social science curriculum improvement in the late fifties and sixties that was sparked by Sputnik, and on teacher education in the mid sixties and early seventies that stemmed from the Great Society's concern for teaching the disadvantaged, left no permanent impact. When federal dollars ceased to flow to universities, their interest in reform waned—it was easier to teach Homer! The effectiveness of community organizations in this area was diminished, because they, too, had been lured by easy dollars. I firmly believe that today's environment for change is a very different one.
>
> The spate of alarming reports by study commissions and individual researchers; the forceful lobbying for funding by teachers' and administrators' unions and by school boards; the rapid increase in state governmental initiatives in seeking educational improvement through goal setting, regulation, and increased resources; the argument over the effectiveness of community empowerment as the path to school improvement; and the willing, if cautious, involvement of business through gifts and technical assistance—these are all attempts to respond to the crisis. We have the possibility to effect change because *all* sectors of society are aroused and ready to become partners in the effort. We can therefore approach today's crisis with a measure of optimism [1987, p. 1].

The federal government should welcome these partners, for they reflect a new kind of American empiricism, an extrapolation of traditional American volunteerism. Indeed, the federal government should seize the opportunity and act as its catalytic leader.

Although the government initiated the first wave of reform by establishing a Commission on Excellence, which issued *A Nation at Risk* in 1983, it has not really pursued the recommendations of that report aggressively. There has been the provocative essay, *To Reclaim a Legacy* (Bennett, 1984), which is severely critical of the curriculum in higher education, and occasional statements about teaching values. There have been annual conferences in Washington devoted to college-school partnerships, conducted by Thomas Evans and Susan Otterburg, and these have been informative. Called "Partnerships in Education," they are sponsored by the Presidential Board of Advisers on Private Sector Initiatives. However, they have not resulted in focused leadership on a sustained basis. Educational reform has been left to the states and has often been effective; but one can make a compelling case that the moment has arrived for federal legislation in support of educational partnerships. Just as the establishment of the National Science Foundation, the National Endowment for the Humanities, and the National Endowment for the Arts has resulted in significant strengthening of the fields they represent, a federal program for college-school collaboration would give national leadership to the many collaborations that have developed from local need and could have, as part of its mandate, challenge grants to businesses, communities, schools and, especially, colleges. It could draft its mandate so that colleges and universities become the leading force in fostering educational partnerships.

The second wave of educational reform will demand the coherent leadership of colleges and universities, for, as Newman (1987) reminds us, its focus will be on higher education as well as on elementary and secondary; on the at-risk student in earlier levels of school but also on the high percentage of dropouts in college; on creating "a climate in the schools that is less

hierarchical, more involving, more exciting, more effective'';
on dealing with the ''linkage points'' between schools and colleges; on assessing the quality of undergraduate education.

Business leaders, governors, and legislators will insist on
knowing what they are paying for in public education—and not
because they are in favor of narrow career education but because
they advocate a fundamental liberal arts education and recognize
it as the only way in which a nation at risk can compete inter-
nationally and assert global leadership. They endorse the fundamental values of educators and are far less vocationally oriented
in their view of American education than are foreign business-
people in relationship to their own school systems, but they want
accountability. The second wave of reform will address the crisis
of minorities in the inner cities, as they work their way through
our commonly shared system of education and demand their
inclusion in our mutual estate. And, finally, it will deal with
the growing teacher shortage in the nation. The number of students is rising in elementary and secondary schools so there will
be a need for more teachers at the same time that resignations
and retirements will occur.

These then are the three fundamental crises that will inform the next stage of educational reform: international competitiveness, opportunities for minorities, and the shortage of
teachers on all levels. They can be confronted most effectively
by educational partnerships that will bring government, business, and the community far closer to schools and colleges than
they have ever been. One can see the convergence of interests
occurring already as commentators remind us of America's poor
educational report card in comparison with that of other coun-
tries, as demographers remind us of population trends, as leaders
of school systems and colleges are chosen, and as salaries of
teachers are negotiated dramatically upwards. The real need
now is to develop productive partnerships in which the constituents respect and trust each other and keep their independent
roles clear. Together they can resolve these crises; separated,
they will contribute only to the continued atomization of schooling in America.

Each of the major constituencies benefits from participation in a partnership not only through the specific ways I have mentioned but also through ways that are difficult to measure. Self-interest will lead to sharing and then to service and, if successful, to a trust among educators at all levels of schooling.

We can already see the future direction of educational partnerships. That future rests primarily with colleges and universities willing to assert leadership in initiating these partnerships. A program such as the Bay Area Writing Project has moved within the past fifteen years from a local success to replication throughout the states. The National Faculty, the Academic Alliance Movement, and the Woodrow Wilson National Fellowship Foundation Institutes have experienced similar expansion. The National Network for Educational Renewal is now in place and has secured the cooperation of twelve state universities and their local schools. As it becomes more visible in the next few years, it will undoubtedly dramatize the impact that college-school collaborations can have in creating coherence in American education.

The SUNY Purchase–Westchester School Partnership is one model that can be replicated by state colleges and universities together with their neighboring schools, businesses, communities, and governmental agencies. It is grounded, like the other collaborations, in the fundamental belief that a partnership is a process, not a product. Emerging from enlightened self-interest, educational partnerships have already become a necessity in most localities—chosen, not mandated, and offering the powerful promise of reform. Wisely organized, a partnership strengthens each culture it encompasses—college, school, business, community, and government—and creates a new and broader culture of mutual concern for the improvement of learning in America. It has taken two hundred years for the country to reach this beginning, but the future of education is now a partnership for the entire society to share. A mutual estate. Our mutual estate.

~~~~~~

Directors and Addresses of Partnerships Cited in This Book

A comprehensive listing of educational partnerships has been assembled by Franklin Wilbur, Leo M. Albert, and M. Jean Young, under the title *The National Directory of School-College Partnerships: Current Models and Practices*. It was sponsored by the National Association of Secondary School Principals, the American Association for Higher Education, and Syracuse University Project Advance and published by the American Association for Higher Education, Washington, D.C., in 1987. It lists more than 1,000 college-school collaborations. The following list includes the partnerships mentioned in this book:

Academic Alliances, 210 Logan Hall/CN, Philadelphia, Pennsylvania 19104. Claire Gaudiani, director. (215) 898-6843.

Advanced Placement Program, College Board, 45 Columbus Avenue, New York, New York 10023-6917. Donald Stewart, president. (212) 713-8000.

Boston Compact, 110 Tremont Street, Boston, Massachusetts. Edward Dooley, executive director. (617) 726-6200.

Center for Educational Renewal, University of Washington, Seattle, Washington 98195. John Goodlad, director. (206) 543-6230.

Center for Excellence in Education, 7710 Old Springhouse Road, McLean, Virginia 22101. Joann DiGennaro, executive director. (703) 448-9062.

Cities in School, Inc., 1023 15th Street, NW Washington, D.C. 20005. William Milliken, president. (202) 861-0230.

The College Board, 45 Columbus Avenue, New York, New York 10023-6917. Donald M. Stewart, president. (212) 713-8000.

National Faculty, 1676 Clifton Road, Atlanta, Georgia 30322. Benjamin Ladner, president. (404) 727-5788.

National Writing Project, 5627 Tolman Hall, School of Education, Berkeley, California 94720. James Gray, director. (415) 642-0963.

New York City Partnership, Inc., 200 Madison Avenue, New York, New York 10016. Frank Macchiarola, president. (212) 561-2000.

Project Advance, 113 Euclid Avenue, Syracuse, New York 13210. Franklin Wilbur, director. (315) 423-2404.

Public Education Fund, 600 Grant Street, Suite 4444, Pittsburgh, Pennsylvania 15219. David Bergholz, director. (412) 281-1890.

Woodrow Wilson National Fellowship Foundation, Princeton, New Jersey. Caroline Wilson, director. (609) 924-4636.

Yale–New Haven Teachers Institute, Box 3563, Yale Station, New Haven, Connecticut. James Vivian, director. (203) 436-3316.

Organization and Content of the SUNY Purchase Westchester School Partnership

Although descriptions of the SUNY Purchase Westchester School Partnership are interwoven throughout this book, a brief history of its development will be useful. This chronology indicates how a rather complex enterprise can be organized within four years.

Chronology of Main Events

August 1983. The American Can Company invites SUNY Purchase to submit a five-year proposal in support of local schools. It suggests possible funding of $500,000 but ultimately contributes $240,000. Eleven school districts join the partnership; their superintendents, together with four college administrators, constitute the steering committee. The dean of liberal arts and sciences is elected chairperson. By April 1984 the five-year proposal has been accepted.

April 1984. At a breakfast meeting on April 24, 1984, formation of the SUNY Purchase Westchester School Partnership is announced to the community of educators, government representatives, and business leaders.

April 1984. An executive director is chosen from 130 applicants. A process evaluator is also chosen. He will be accountable to the donor and work with the partnership.

July 1984. A proposal writer is put on retainer and will develop all proposals in consultation with the executive director.

October 1984. A Math/Science Resource and Computer Training Center is funded by the State Education Department. Located in the Division of Natural Sciences at SUNY Purchase, it has an autonomous twenty-one-member policy board and is affiliated with the partnership. It will concentrate on elementary science.

May 1985. Six new Westchester County school districts are admitted to the partnership.

July 1985. Weeklong institutes in chemistry and mathematics, sponsored by the Woodrow Wilson National Fellowship Foundation, are offered to sixty teachers. In July 1986, institutes in physics and a locally developed earth science institute are added; 120 teachers attend four institutes. In July 1987, institutes in chemistry, mathematics, physics, writing, and earth science are offered; the first four are duplicated for New York City teachers. Three hundred teachers attend nine institutes. Follow-up sessions are conducted throughout the academic year.

November 1985. An IBM loaned executive, who helped to conduct the corporation's Education Executive Program, adapts that program to the partnership—renamed Workshops for Educator Leadership Development (Project WELD)—and leads eleven workshops, together with the executive director and a superintendent, for the academic year. He is replaced by another IBM loaned executive in May 1987, and a Center for Leadership Development is established.

July 1986. Four new districts are admitted to the partnership to bring the total to twenty-one. Districts begin to support the partnership through annual dues—a total of $55,000.

July 1986. An Institute in Motivation, a Fellowship Program for Guidance Counselors, and a Center for Economic Education are initiated. More than eighty teachers take part in their activities.

September 1986. Three additional positions are granted to

SUNY Purchase: a director of the Center for Mathematics and Science, an assistant to the center, and an administrative assistant to the partnership.

September 1986. Students from local school districts are selected to participate in "Revolutions in Western Thought," a freshman great books course at SUNY Purchase.

February 1987. Five seminars are offered by the college's social science division during the spring semester. These seminars are based on the current research activities of the faculty.

April 1987. A statewide conference for colleges, schools, and businesses is held to replicate the partnership. In addition to national speakers—Ernest Boyer, Frank Newman, William Woodside, Harold Hodgkinson, and Floretta McKenzie—leaders of major partnerships make presentations.

June 1987. A program for retired executives is established.

June 1987. A program for at-risk students is initiated in New Rochelle High School, with linkages established to the Governor's School and the Business Alliance.

July 1987. Institutes in foreign languages and esthetic education are started, and institutes in writing/literature are planned.

July 1987. The executive director resigns, and a new director begins the second phase of the partnership.

Figure 1. Organizational Chart

SUNY Purchase Westchester School Partnership.

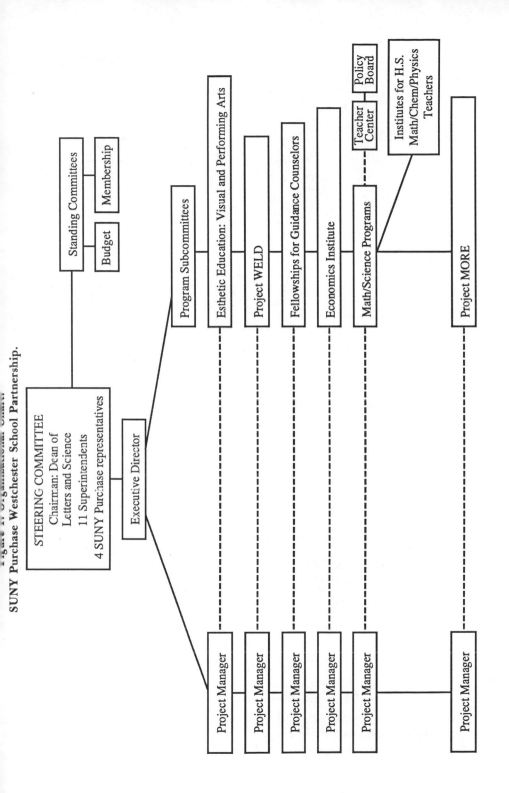

Table 1. Funding Formula for Districts:
SUNY Purchase Westchester School Partnership.

1987–88 School Year (Base Rate = $1.60)

Districts	Per-Pupil Expenditure	Ratio	Number of Students	Total Charge	Per-Pupil Charge
	A	A ÷ 10,596		$	$
Abbott UFSD[a]	17,968	—	204	500	—
Ardsley[b]	9,663	0.91	1,349	1,964	1.46
Bedford[bc]	10,188	0.96	3,008	4,229	1.41
Blind Brook–Rye	8,633	0.81	916	1,187	1.30
Briarcliff	10,355	0.98	990	1,552	1.57
Byram Hills	9,437	0.89	1,582	2,253	1.42
Chappaqua[b]	7,687	0.73	3,584	3,553	0.99
Dobbs Ferry	8,844	0.83	955	1,268	1.33
Eastchester[b]	10,012	0.94	1,744	2,623	1.50
Edgemont-Greenburgh	9,064	0.86	1,386	1,907	1.38
Harrison	8,842	0.83	2,251	2,989	1.33
Irvington[b]	9,544	0.90	1,124	1,619	1.44
Katonah-Lewisboro	8,376	0.79	2,692	3,281	1.22
Lakeland[b]	8,359	0.79	5,519	4,903	0.89
Mamaroneck	9,713	0.92	3,781	4,623	1.22
Mt. Pleasant	7,695	0.73	1,601	1,870	1.17
Mt. Vernon	6,296	0.59	9,558	4,372	0.46
New Rochelle	7,779	0.73	7,441	5,112	0.69
Pelham	8,212	0.78	1,791	2,235	1.25
Pleasantville[b]	8,811	0.83	1,132	1,503	1.33
Port Chester–Rye	6,741	0.64	2,609	2,615	1.00
Public Schools of the Tarrytowns	9,325	0.88	1,937	2,720	1.41
Rye	8,891	0.84	1,906	2,562	1.34
Rye Neck	9,106	0.86	928	1,277	1.38
White Plains	10,596	1.00	5,136	6,053	1.18
Yonkers	7,093	0.67	18,485	6,106	0.33
Total/Average				$74,876	1.20

[a]This district was established by a special act of the New York State legislature. It serves 250–300 students, all of whom have experienced difficulties in school and most of whom have some form of social trauma in their background. Because of its anomalous status, the per-pupil expenditure was higher than in other districts, and the Steering Committee agreed to charge a flat fee of $500 for its annual dues.
[b]District statistics not confirmed
[c]Pending board approval

Individual Programs

The following summaries of the six major projects in the SUNY Purchase Westchester School Partnership provide brief descriptions of their origins, goals, activities, evaluations, finances, and future trends. These descriptions have been written by Resa Fremed, former executive director of the partnership, and Richard Wing, proposal writer.

The Mathematics/Science Teacher Resources and Training Center. In the spring of 1984 the newly formed partnership applied for and received a grant from New York State for the establishment of a Teacher Center that would help elementary-level teachers improve their skills in teaching mathematics and science and in using computers as an educational tool. The center also planned to set up a resource facility where local teachers could meet and obtain materials of instruction, library references, computer programs, videotapes, and other resources for the teaching of science and mathematics.

During the first year a grant of $30,000 enabled the project to recruit a core faculty of six instructors who would subsequently help train a number of peer teachers. These peer teachers would then lead groups of other elementary teachers in activities to strengthen their skills in the teaching of science and math. During the first year a conference was held in the spring, and the policy board held regular meetings, with Blind Brook–Rye School District serving as the local educational agency.

The second-year budget of $115,000 enabled the Teacher Center to hire a full-time director, Susan Cook, and to organize a second conference and give workshops for the twenty-four selected peer teachers. Seventy teachers and ten administrators attended the conference, participating in sessions on astronomy and meteorology and hearing a presentation on the New York State science curriculum. The administrators attended a meeting on the subject of staff development. During the 1985–86 school year the peer teachers attended a series of five workshops on the topics of electricity, magnetism, states of matter, chemical reactions, and concepts in the life sciences. In June there was also a seminar in staff development for principals and teachers from eight districts. All workshops were evaluated through analysis of responses on questionnaires administered to participants. The analysis shows a uniformly high level of approval on the part of those in attendance. A follow-up questionnaire indicated that the peers had begun to introduce some units from the workshops into their classes and to document interactions with other colleagues.

In 1986–87 the pattern of conference, workshop, and supplemental activities was repeated. In addition, the project has added the services of a part-time computer specialist and has established a minigrant program in which over $9,000 in awards have been granted to teachers for sixteen small educational projects. A new conference, one on math and computer usage, was held in the spring of 1987, and additional activities are under way for college students who are interested in learning more about teaching science as a profession. An "outreach" program has also been initiated to supplement the peer workshops.

The resource center of the project has been steadily accumulating instructional materials and equipment. Several new computers have been added to bring the total to twelve, and the number of teachers visiting the center is growing.

For the future, a three-year plan has been put together for the state by project staff and the policy board, which consists now of fourteen school districts, SUNY Purchase delegates, partnership staff, parents, and members of the business community. As required by the State Teacher Center Guidelines, a majority of the policy board members are teachers representing their professional organizations. The new plan calls for expansion of services to teachers and enlargement of district membership. To date, the center has been funded primarily by the state, with grants of $30,000 (1984–85), $115,000 (1985–86), $150,000 (1986–87), and $225,000 (1987–88). Unless there is a considerable increase in the size of state grants over the next three years, however, it will not be possible to offer some of the proposed new activities. For that reason the board is exploring prospects for additional funding by foundations and other external organizations.

Center for Mathematics and Science Education. The Center for Mathematics and Science Education offers a number of programs intended to improve the teaching of science in secondary schools of the region. Goals include the extension of this service to gifted students, to female and minority students who may undertake careers in science, and to students in high school science classes who can profit from working in the well-equipped laboratories of SUNY Purchase.

Most activities of the center take place in the facilities of the natural science building at SUNY Purchase and are under the general direction of Carlo Parravano, associate professor of chemistry. An advisory committee composed of high school science teachers, college faculty and administrators, and school superintendents has recently been established to provide guidance to the center.

The principal project of the center to date has been a set of summer institutes for secondary-level math and science teachers. As a satellite of the Woodrow Wilson National Fellowship Foundation Program, the center sponsored two institutes, in chemistry and mathematics, during the second week of July 1985 for fifty-nine teachers. These sessions were taught by master teachers who had been trained in Princeton, New Jersey, by the Woodrow Wilson Foundation, and the institute presented curriculum materials prepared by that foundation. In 1986 chemistry and math institutes were again offered, as well as a new session in physics and a two-week earth science workshop that was developed in Westchester by a Briarcliff High School science teacher. One hundred and twenty-nine teachers attended the four workshops, and many of them took part in follow-up workshops offered periodically through the 1986–87 school year. In the summer of 1987 more than three hundred teachers attended ten workshops in physics, chemistry, mathematics, and earth science. Assessment of these institutes has shown them to be extremely well received by participants on the basis of quality and relevance to their teaching.

In addition to the summer institutes, the center has initiated a program under which high school classes in science visit SUNY Purchase, make use of the laboratories there, and attend lectures on topics in science.

The institute program of the center for secondary teachers is complemented by the activities of the Teacher Center, described in the previous section, with its science and computer programs for elementary schoolteachers.

The Woodrow Wilson Foundation has negotiated an agreement with the New York City Board of Education whereby the center at SUNY Purchase will repeat sponsorship of four additional summer institutes in 1988 in chemistry, mathematics, physics, and earth science for New York City teachers.

The summer institutes have received support from the Economic Education Security Act, IBM, various foundations, local school district fees, and the State University of New York. A major four-year proposal has been approved by the National Science Foundation.

Workshops for Educator Leadership Development (Project WELD). This is a program consisting of two-day workshops on effective leadership, understanding people, and communications skills. The rationale for this kind of project has been expressed by the U.S. Department of Education, LEAD Program, in these terms: "The growing body of knowledge about 'effective schools' consistently pointed to the key role of administrators in such schools . . . and long-standing and recent research on educational reform and school improvement programs confirms that success may be largely dependent upon skilled administrators . . . . Yet current practices for training, selecting, and rewarding school administrators do not always identify and develop needed competence" (Fremed and Wing, 1986, p. 9).

Convinced of the need for applying Project WELD to local school management, over two hundred administrators from districts in the area attended the series of workshops offered by the project during the spring of 1986. Each workshop lasted for two days, stressing leadership theory the first day and dealing with understanding people, communication networks, and selected critical issues the second. Attendance at each session was limited to about twenty executives, including some from the business community.

The workshops were conducted by Robert A. Eberle, who has been an executive with IBM for twenty-five years. His services were made available to the partnership for the purpose of running the leadership series, which is modeled on the highly successful IBM Education Executive Program in Southbury, Connecticut. This program has hosted 1,300 administrators from 500 school districts throughout the United States since its beginning in 1984. It was also conducted in Hong Kong and Singapore for education executives and received extremely high ratings there, according to information released by IBM.

Local evaluation of Project WELD confirms the reputation that it had before becoming a partnership activity. Questionnaires on the quality and usefulness of the workshops are returned with uniformly high ratings; a number of participants have written letters of praise to the partnership administration. Word spread by local superintendents who have already attended the workshops has persuaded many others to enroll.

Bob Eberle retired in June of 1987. In his place IBM assigned William Langenstein who is now at work planning a new executive leadership project to be called WELD II.

Fellowship Program for Secondary School Guidance Counselors. The guidance counselor project has as its purpose to strengthen secondary school guidance functions by helping selected counselors increase their knowledge of working conditions in local industries, learn more about job opportunities in the area, and improve the educational preparation of students for entry into the employment market.

The program is also intended to benefit participating businesses and industries by providing better training and orientation for those students who will seek employment in local firms and by giving employers new insights into the occupational training practices of local districts.

The fellowship program is now in the third of three phases that form the framework of each year's operations:

Phase I involves a spring series of seminars for counselors and is cosponsored by the Institute for Applied Economics. In the 1986 spring program the topics of these seminars included review of the regional labor market, insurance occupations, health care, computers, advertising, entrepreneurship, finance, communications, international business, and hotel occupations.

Phase II provides for monthlong summer employment of counselors in local businesses. Summer 1986 employers included banks, personnel services, electronics firms, data-processing firms, and a chemical product distributor. Nine counselors completed the summer internships.

Phase III emphasizes yearlong projects designed and conducted by project participants for the purpose of applying the summer experiences in the counselors' schools. Sample projects are bank-teller training, preparation for civil service jobs, exploration of job opportunities in Westchester County, and direct exposure to entry-level employment.

The participants in this project are all counselors at the secondary school level, employed by partnership schools, and committed to remaining in their jobs during the school year following the summer fellowship. Fellows are paid $2,700 each. Revenues come from cooperating firms ($2,500) and from the school districts ($1,000) where the fellows are employed. It was originally planned that these sources of income would be sufficient to cover expenses, but they have turned out to be inadequate to pay for the necessary support services of the first year. Additional funds are therefore being sought to cover these basic costs, as well as the expense of changes and improvements in operation recommended by the project's advisory council, such as organizing a Career Information Exchange for the counselors, issuing *The Handbook for Career Opportunities in Westchester County,* and providing continued support in the form of materials and services for the first wave of fellows during the second year of the project.

The first year of the project has been observed and assessed by the project evaluator, who summarized her conclusions in the following way: "Counselor participants generally gave this first pilot year for the fellowship program excellent to good ratings on the formal evaluation instrument . . . . The majority of employers [attending] an all-day meeting October 2, 1986, expressed enthusiasm for their summer experience with their counselor, and underscored the need for and the value of such programs." With such encouragement the partnership has continued to move forward with plans for the future.

Center for Economic Education. It is widely recognized that an understanding of economic principles is important if the student and later the adult citizen is to handle personal finances, to find an occupation and succeed in it, and to deal with complex political and social problems, as well as those that are primarily economic. Yet the schools and other educational agencies of the community have not given this subject sufficient emphasis. Recognizing this need, the New York State Education Department has issued a regulation requiring completion of at least a one-semester course in economics as a prerequisite to graduation from New York State secondary schools, starting in 1989. This requirement will oblige local school districts to hire or retrain large numbers of teachers in order to offer sufficient classes in economics. There is also the need to introduce economics into the lower grades.

Aware of the lack of qualified economics teachers, the partnership and SUNY Purchase faculty last year established a Center for Economic Education under the direction of Peter Bell, associate professor of economics at the college. The center is assisted by the JCEE and thus becomes one of 270 national centers in this field. The center is dedicated to improving economics education through teacher training, to articulating high school and college curricula in economics, to assisting the school districts to comply with the New York State Regents' requirements for completion by all students of a course in economics, to forming links with business and community, to establishing a resource library of instructional resources and other services for economic education—housed at SUNY—and to operating a series of summer institutes in which master teachers will be prepared to instruct other social studies teachers as the need increases.

The first such institute was held daily from July 7 through July 11, 1986. Principal lecturers were Peter Bell and Kimberly Christensen from SUNY, aided in the application of economic concepts to the curriculum by Roland O'Neal, director of curriculum in the Lakeland School District. Subjects included a review of economic theory as expounded by Smith, Keynes, and Marx; current economic policy; techniques of teaching economics; and the introduction to materials and other resources of the Developmental Economics Education Program (DEEP). Forty secondary schoolteachers from a total of sixteen districts participated in the institute. Responses of teachers to an evaluative questionnaire were generally quite enthusiastic, with many expressions of satisfaction with the institute and numerous suggestions on improving future programs and adapting them to the varying needs of participants.

Two summer institute follow-up sessions have been held, and a lecture series was begun under the sponsorship of the center. This series offered six lectures on the subject of internal debt and the world economy, with such distinguished speakers as Jorge Sol, former minister of finance of El Salvador.

The center has produced a five-year plan, projecting extension of economics education in the school progressively through grades 12, 9 to 11, 7 to 8, and 1 to 6, with a gradually expanding number of master teachers and others trained by the center. Although the center has received support from the JCEE and the State Council on Economic Education, as well as from two corporate foundations, including $20,000 recently committed by American Express, it will need additional funds to meet the expenses estimated at $29,000 (plus indirect costs); $53,000 in 1988–89; and $55,000 in 1989–90. These monies will support administration of the center as it expands to improve economic education in the schools, college, and community.

Motivational Opportunities to Reach Excellence (Project MORE). The intent of this project is to identify instructional strategies for increasing student willingness to learn and to encourage elementary teachers to put these strategies into practice with the expectation that students will show increased interest in learning as a result. Expected outcomes are these:

- As the project progresses, the teachers will become increasingly concerned with the *impact* of their instructional practices on their pupils.
- There will be a significant increase in the *use* of motivational strategies by teachers by the end of the project.

The principal activity to date has been an intensive eight-day institute held during the month of July 1986 at SUNY Purchase and attended by ten teachers and five principals representing five school districts in Southern Westchester: Harrison, Mt. Vernon, New Rochelle, Port Chester, and the Tarrytowns. Instructors at the institute were Raymond Wlodkowski of the University of Wisconsin; Ruth Greenblatt, a Port Chester elementary school principal; Robert Eberle of IBM; Angela Kalavis of St. John's University; and Deborah Roody from the Network in Andover, Massachusetts. Their topics included motivational strategies, learning styles, leadership theory, and practical application of learning psychology to the classroom.

When asked to assess the quality and usefulness of the summer institute, responding participants gave it an average rating of 4.7 on a scale of 1 (low) to 5 (high) and added numerous compliments on the value of the experience. They also stated that they looked forward to the bimonthly follow-up sessions scheduled during the 1986–87 school year.

As part of the second-year plan, a four-week school located at the Purchase School for sixty fourth- or fifth-grade students will be organized to allow project teachers and administrators to apply principles of motivation, previously identified during 1986–87, to classroom situations. During this session, which was held in July 1987, Project MORE staff engaged in team teaching, intense study, and discussion of motivational principles and procedures. The outcome of this form of training will encourage significant growth on the part of both principals and teachers in their ability to apply motivating tactics for the benefit of their pupils.

It is hypothesized that by the end of the second project year, participating teachers will change their behavior from a focus on "self" to a focus on "task" and "impact on students." A second objective is for the teachers to change their levels of use from "nonuse" to "mechanical use" to "routine use" of motivational strategies in the effort to stimulate greater interest in school on the part of presently unmotivated students.

As its contribution to the payment of project expenses, each of the five participating districts has paid $2,500 during the first year. Budgeted costs for the second year run to $42,000, of which the major portion must be obtained from external sources. Several foundations are being approached in an effort to obtain supportive grants. A New York legislative grant of $23,000 has recently been committed to this project.

Arguments in Support
of Educational Partnerships

During the organization and development of the SUNY Purchase Westchester School Partnership, I have met with numerous representatives of school boards, faculty administrators in colleges, and leaders of corporations. The recurring question raised by each of these constituents is "Why join an educational partnership?" The following responses may be helpful to others who encounter this same fundamental question.

How Will Joining an Educational
Partnership Benefit a School District?

1. *Achieving fiscal savings.* A partnership allows a school district to combine resources with other districts and the college involved to provide services it cannot offer alone.

2. *Gaining greater supplementary funding.* The partnership presents to corporations and foundations a funding proposal that is more focused and larger than any a single district can submit.

3. *Improving professionalism for teachers.* A teacher in a small school district, who may be alone in his or her discipline, will be able to meet counterparts in other schools and be reinvigorated professionally.

4. *Attaining freedom from bureaucracy.* Because of its freedom from state education department constraints, a partnership allows its leaders to experiment with and develop new programs far more rapidly than they could otherwise.

5. *Establishing personal ownership.* Superintendents shape the educational agenda.

6. *Achieving integration with the college or university.* School districts have an integrated relationship with the college or university so that teachers can participate in research and other activities.

7. *Enhancing facilities.* College facilities such as science and language laboratories can augment the necessarily limited facilities of a school district.

8. *Networking.* Through the network and combined resources of other school districts and the college, partnership educators are kept current with the latest developments in their disciplines.

9. *Engendering community support.* By joining a partnership, school districts make a compelling case for further support of their own districts.

10. *Improving prestige for superintendents.* By heading partnerships, superintendents gain visibility as educational leaders.

How Will Joining or Sponsoring an Educational Partnership Benefit a College?

1. *Increasing recruitment.* By bringing teachers and students to the college, the partnership encourages enrollment.

2. *Strengthening the funding base through public service.* By serving schools, colleges will persuade community leaders to be supportive of their efforts to raise funds from both the public and private sectors.

3. *Shaping educational goals.* As college leaders work with their high school counterparts, they can establish clear goals and gain increased control over the curriculum.

4. *Improving faculty compensation.* Insofar as faculty members lead projects, they receive additional compensation. The partnership also provides an audience for a speaker's bureau.

5. *Enhancing pedagogical and curricular interaction.* Faculty members can focus more directly on teaching strategies than they tend to at the college level.

6. *Revealing teachers as motivated students.* Through partnership institutes and courses, faculty members are exposed to and

impressed by the high motivation and intelligence of high school teachers.

7. *Providing research opportunities.* Faculty members see that the school districts offer opportunities for personal research: sociologists for drop-out prevention programs; scientists in science education; psychologists for early childhood development programs, and so forth.

8. *Providing educational leadership to a community.* By working with educators in the schools, college faculty become leaders of individual disciplines.

9. *Leveraging school and corporate support to attract more state funding.* Garnering the support of schools and corporations makes colleges' cases for increased support from the state compelling. Colleges in partnerships can justify funding requests to support not only their own programs but also their contributions to their communities.

10. *Funding of additional state positions.* As the need for directors becomes evident, the college can request state positions and in the process augment its own faculty. The director of a science or economics center teaches on the faculty and also administers the program, and the justification is that he or she now is an educational leader within the community.

How Will Joining an Educational Partnership Benefit a Corporation?

1. *Focusing donations.* The corporation focuses its donations and need not distribute small amounts to competing school districts.

2. *Improving public relations.* The image of the corporation as a friendly community citizen is enhanced.

3. *Attracting current and future employees.* By contributing to partnership programs, the corporation improves the schools that educate the children of its employees and makes those schools seem more appealing to future employees.

4. *Setting an educational agenda.* Through its support, the corporation furnishes seed money for educational programs it feels ought to be developed further.

5. *Humanizing funding.* Rather than contribute support to a faceless government, the corporate sector funds programs to which it can relate specifically.

6. *Creating a "unified voice" to influence legislation.* By supporting specific projects, corporations exert pressure on government for further funding.

7. *Developing better human resources.* Corporations help to educate students who may be their future employees.

8. *Reducing welfare and unemployment costs to all citizens.* It is more cost effective to support educational programs than to pay for welfare and unemployment.

9. *Addressing the needs of minority and disadvantaged students.* As urban centers become increasingly populated by minority and disadvantaged students, corporations can help provide educational opportunities.

10. *Providing role models for students.* Through greater interaction with the schools, business executives can serve as role models for students and attract them into the business community.

References

Adler, M. J. *The Paideia Proposal: An Educational Manifesto*. New York: Macmillan, 1982.

Bennett, W. J. *To Reclaim a Legacy*. Washington, D.C.: National Endowment for the Humanities, 1984.

Bennis, W. G. "Conversation with Warren Bennis." *Organizational Dynamics*, 1974, *2*, 51–66.

Bennis, W. G., and Namus, B. *Leaders: The Strategies for Taking Charge*. New York: Harper & Row, 1985.

Bergholz, D. *Public Education Fund*. Pittsburgh: Public Education Fund, 1985.

Blackmer, A. R. *General Education in School and College: A Committee Report by Members of the Faculty of Andover, Exeter, Lawrenceville, Harvard, Princeton, and Yale*. Cambridge, Mass.: Harvard University Press, 1952.

Boyer, E. *High School: A Report on Secondary Education in America*. New York: Harper & Row, 1983.

Boyer, E. "The Need for School-College Collaboration." In J. Rosenblatt (ed.), *Higher Education and National Affairs*. American Council on Higher Education, 1985.

Burns, J. M. *Leadership*. New York: Harper & Row, 1978.

Chance, W. *The Best of Educations: Reforming America's Public Schools in the 1980s*. Chicago: The John D. and Catherine MacArthur Foundation, 1986.

Cleveland, H. *The Knowledge Executive*. New York: Dutton, 1985.

Clinton, H. M. "The Readjustment of Our Fundamental Schools." *University Record,* 1923, *9* (2), 73.

Cohen, S. "Administrative Models: Corporate and Government." In T. L. Gross (ed.), *Our Mutual Estate: Schools/College/Business Partnerships.* Purchase, N.Y.: SUNY Purchase, 1987.

Cohen, S., and Lorentz, E. "Networking: Educational Program Policy for the Late Seventies." *EDC News,* 1977, *10,* 2.

College Board. *Academic Preparation for College: What Students Need to Know and Be Able to Do.* New York: College Board, 1983.

Conant, J. B. *The Education of American Teachers.* New York: McGraw-Hill, 1963.

Cordovea, F. *The Education of Educators.* Seattle: Information Services, University of Washington, 1986.

Cross, K. P. *Beyond the Open Door: New Students to Higher Education.* San Francisco: Jossey-Bass, 1971.

Cross, K. P. *Accent on Learning: Improving Instruction and Reshaping the Curriculum.* San Francisco: Jossey-Bass, 1976.

Danzberger, J. *Summary Program Description for the Year-Long Work/Education of the Institute for Educational Leadership.* Washington, D.C.: Institute for Educational Leadership, 1984.

Desruisseaux, P. "Foundations Are Asked to Help Train and Encourage New Leaders." *Chronicle of Higher Education,* April 30, 1986, p. 19.

Dewey, J. *Democracy in Education.* New York: Free Press, 1916.

DiGennaro, J. *The Admiral H. G. Rickover Foundation.* Leesburg, Va.: Rickover Science Institutes, 1985.

Duke, L. *Beyond Creating: The Place for Art in America's Schools.* Los Angeles: Getty Center for Education in the Arts, 1985.

Eble, K. E. *Professors as Teachers.* San Francisco: Jossey-Bass, 1972.

Eble, K. E. *The Craft of Teaching: A Guide to Mastering the Professor's Art.* San Francisco: Jossey-Bass, 1976.

Eble, K. E. *The Art of Administration: A Guide for Academic Administrators.* San Francisco: Jossey-Bass, 1978.

Eble, K. E. *The Aims of College Teaching.* San Francisco: Jossey-Bass, 1983.

Eisner, E. W. *The Role of Discipline-Based Art Education in America's Schools.* Los Angeles: Getty Center for Education in the Arts, 1987.

Ericksen, S. C. *Motivation for Learning.* Ann Arbor: University of Michigan Press, 1974.

Ericksen, S. C. *The Essence of Good Teaching: Helping Students Learn and Remember What They Learn.* San Francisco: Josscy-Bass, 1984.

Eurich, N. *Corporate Classrooms: The Learning Business.* Princeton, N.J.: The Carnegie Foundation for the Advancement of Teaching, 1985.

Fortune, R. (ed.) *School-College Collaboration Programs.* New York: Modern Language Association, 1986.

Freeman, F. H., Gregory R., and Clark, M. B. *Leadership Education: A Source Book.* Greensboro, N.C.: Center for Creative Leadership, 1987.

Fremed, R., and Wing, R. W. *Third Annual Report–1986.* Purchase, N.Y.: SUNY Purchase Westchester School Partnership, 1986.

Gardner, J. *Leadership: A Sample of the Wisdom of John Gardner.* Minneapolis: University of Minnesota Press, 1981.

Gardner, J. *Excellence.* New York: Norton, 1984.

Gardner, J. *Leadership Papers.* Washington, D.C.: Leadership Studies Program, 1986.

Gaudiani, C., and Burnett, D. *Academic Alliances: A New Approach to School-College Collaboration.* Washington, D.C.: American Association of Higher Education, 1986.

Gifford, B. "Should We Abolish the Bachelor's Degree in Education?" *Change,* Sept./Oct., 1986, pp. 31–36.

Goldberg, P. "Administrative Models: Corporate and Government." In T. L. Gross (ed.), *Our Mutual Estate: Schools/College/Business Partnerships.* Purchase, N.Y.: SUNY Purchase Westchester School Partnership, 1987.

Goodlad, J. I. *A Place Called School: Prospects for the Future.* New York: McGraw-Hill, 1984.

Goodlad, J. I. *The National Network for Educational Renewal.* Seattle: The Center for Educational Renewal Institute for Policy

Studies in Education, University of Washington, 1986.

Gray, J. "University of California, Berkeley: The Bay Area Writing Project and the National Writing Project." In R. Fortune (ed.), *School-College Collaboration Programs*. New York: Modern Language Association, 1986.

Greene, M. "On Defining Aesthetic Education." *Lincoln Center Institute Report*, Summer 1985, pp. 1, 11.

Gross, T. L. (ed.) *Our Mutual Estate: School/College/Business Partnerships*. Purchase, N.Y.: SUNY Purchase, 1987.

"Guidelines Set for New Program to Improve School Leadership." *Federal Register*, Sept. 18, 1986, p. 33218.

Hahn, A., and Danzberger, J. *Dropouts in America: Enough is Known for Action—A Report for Policy Makers and Grants Makers*. Washington, D.C.: Institute for Educational Leadership, 1987.

Hall, B. "Youth Program Tackles Nation's Truancy and Dropout Problems." *Christian Science Monitor*, June 23, 1986.

Hanson, H. "Twenty-Five Years of the Advanced Placement Program: Encouraging Able Students." *The College Board Review*, 1980, *115*, pp. 8–12, 35.

Hechinger, F. "When Things Go Wrong." *New York Times*, Mar. 24, 1987a, p. B8.

Hechinger, F. "Leadership for Schools." *New York Times*, Aug. 25, 1987b, p. C11.

Hersey, P., and Blanchard, K. H. *Management of Organizational Behavior: Utilizing Human Resources*. Englewood Cliffs, N.J.: Prentice Hall, 1982.

Hodgkinson, H. L. *All One System*. Washington, D.C.: Institute for Educational Leadership, 1985.

Hodgkinson, H. L. "Perspectives on Partnerships: Future." In T. L. Gross (ed.), *Our Mutual Estate: Schools/College/Business Partnerships*. Purchase, N.Y.: SUNY Purchase, 1987.

Howe, H. *Keeping the Options Open: Final Report of the Commission on Precollege Guidance and Counseling*. New York: College Board, 1986.

Hunter, M. "Issue Issue Issue Issue:." [sic] *ASCD Update*, November, 1984, p. 4.

Hunter, M. *Motivation Theory for Teachers, A Programmed Book*. El Segundo, Calif.: TIP Publications, 1985a.

Hunter, M. *Prescription for Improved Instruction and Mastery Teaching.* El Segundo, Calif.: TIP Publications, 1985b.

Illich, I. *Deschooling Society.* New York: Harper & Row, 1970.

Jennings, E. E. *An Anatomy of Leadership: Princes, Heroes, and Supermen.* New York: Harper & Row, 1960.

Johns Hopkins University. *Reclaiming the Future: A Liberal Arts Education for Highly Able Youth.* Baltimore, Md.: Center for the Advancement of Academically Talented Youth, Johns Hopkins University, 1986.

Joint Council for Economic Education (JCEE). *Development of Economic Education Program.* New York: JCEE, 1986.

Knox, A. *Science and Mathematics Master Teacher Centers 1986.* Princeton, N.J.: Woodrow Wilson National Fellowship Foundation, 1986.

Kotter, J. P. "Power, Dependence, and Effective Management." *Harvard Business Review,* 1977, *55,* pp. 125–136.

Ladner, B. *The Humanities in Precollegiate Education.* Chicago: University of Chicago Press, 1984.

Lane, J. J., and Walberg, H. J. *Effective School Leadership.* Berkeley, Calif.: McCutchan, 1987.

Lathrop, J. *The Leadership Development Program.* College Park, Md.: The Center for Leadership Development, 1985.

Lieberman, J. *Middle College: A Ten-Year Study.* New York: LaGuardia Community College, 1986.

McCall, M. *Leaders and Leadership: Of Substance and Shadow.* Technical Report. Greensboro, N.C.: Center for Creative Leadership, 1977.

McClelland, D. C., and Burnham, D. H. "Power Is the Great Motivator." *Harvard Business Review,* 1976, *54,* pp. 38–48.

MacDowell, M. "Foreword." In R. Saunders (ed.), *A Framework for Teaching Basic Concepts.* (2nd ed.) New York: Joint Council for Economic Education, 1984.

McKenzie, F. "Perspectives on Partnerships: Urban Perspective." In T. L. Gross (ed.), *Our Mutual Estate: School/College/Business Partnerships.* Purchase, N.Y.: SUNY Purchase, 1987.

Madeja, S., and Smith, V. "Art Education." *ASCD Curriculum Update,* July 1982, p. 1.

Maeroff, G. *School and College Partnerships in Education*. Princeton,
    N.J.: The Carnegie Foundation for the Advancement of
    Teaching, 1983.
Maeroff, G. "Classical Music Not Their Thing." *New York
    Times,* December 4, 1984, pp. C1, C16.
Mason, B. *Fellowship Program for Secondary School Guidance Coun-
    selors.* Purchase, N.Y.: SUNY Purchase Westchester School
    Partnership, 1986.
Milliken, B. *Cities in Schools: An Overview*. Washington, D.C.:
    Cities in Schools, 1986.
Mix, H. *Motivating the Learner.* Purchase, N.Y.: SUNY Purchase
    Westchester School Partnership, 1985.
Morris, V. C. *Deaning: Middle Management in Academe.* Urbana:
    University of Illinois Press, 1981.
*A Nation Prepared: Teachers for the 21st Century: The Report of the
    Task Force on Teaching as a Profession.* New York: Carnegie Cor-
    poration of New York, 1986.
National Commission on Excellence. *A Nation at Risk: The Im-
    perative for Educational Reform.* Washington, D.C.: Government
    Printing Office, 1983.
National Endowment for the Humanities. *Division of Education
    Programs.* Washington, D.C.: National Endowment for the
    Humanities, 1986.
*The National Faculty: Distinguished Scholars Serving the Nation's
    Schools.* Atlanta, Ga.: National Faculty of Humanities, Arts,
    and Science, 1987.
The National Writing Project: Brochure and Publications for Teachers.
    Berkeley: University of California, Berkeley, Bay Area Writ-
    ing Project, 1987.
Newman, F. "A Perspective of the States." In T. L. Gross (ed.),
    Our Mutual Estate: Schools/College/Business Partnerships. Purchase,
    N.Y.: SUNY Purchase, 1987.
Nord, W. P. "Developments in the Study of Power." In M.
    Gruneberg and T. Wall (eds.), *Social Psychology and Organiza-
    tional Behavior.* New York: Wiley, 1984.
Olson, L. "Schools, Universities in 10 States Have Joined
    Goodlad's 'Network for Educational Renewal'." *Education
    Week,* April 30, 1986, pp. 1, 16.

Olson, L. "Network for Renewal: Goodlad Seeks Stronger School-University Alliances." *Education Week,* March 18, 1987, pp. 1, 18, 19, 20.

Pace, F. *Study Finds Vast New Source of Math and Science Teachers to Ease National Crisis.* New York: National Executive Service Corps, 1987.

Parravano, C. *A Center for Mathematics and Science Education: A Proposal to the National Science Foundation, 1987.* Purchase, N.Y.: SUNY Purchase Westchester School Partnership, 1987.

Peters, T. J., and Waterman, R. H. *In Search of Excellence: Lessons from America's Best Run Companies.* New York: Warner, 1985.

Pettigrew, A. M. *The Politics of Organizational Decision Making.* London: Tavistock, 1973.

Powell, S. *Peer Leadership Development Program.* Princeton, N.J.: Princeton Psychological Associates, 1987.

Rallis, S. F., and Highsmith, M. C. "The Myth of the 'Great Principal'." *American Educator,* Spring, 1987.

Ranbom, S. *School Dropouts: Everybody's Problem.* Washington, D.C.: Institute for Educational Leadership, 1986.

Ravitch, D. *The Great School Wars, 1805–1973.* New York: Basic Books, 1974.

Ravitch, D. *The Troubled Crusade: American Education 1945–1980.* New York: Basic Books, 1983.

Reynolds, W. A. "Pride or Prejudice: Teacher Preparation in State Colleges and Universities." In A. W. Oster (ed.), *An Urgent Imperative: Proceedings of the Wingspread Conference on Teacher Preparation.* Washington, D.C.: American Association of State Colleges and Universities, 1984.

Rickover Science Students' Reports. A program of the Admiral H. G. Rickover Foundation. Leesburg, Va.: Rickover Science Institutes, 1985.

Russell, J., and Colletti, C. *Project More: Motivational Opportunities to Reach Excellence.* Purchase, N.Y.: SUNY Purchase Westchester School Partnership, 1986.

Sarason, S. *The Culture of the School and the Problem of Change.* Newton, Mass.: Allyn & Bacon, 1982.

Saunders, P. *A Framework for Teaching the Basic Concepts.* New York: Joint Council for Economic Education, 1984.

Schubart, M. *The Lincoln Center Institute.* New York: Lincoln Center for the Performing Arts, 1986.

Seeley, D. *Education Through Partnership.* Washington, D.C.: American Enterprise for Public Policy Research, 1985.

Shanker, A. "Where We Stand." *New York Times,* May 17, 1987, p. E7.

Sizer, T. R. *Horace's Compromise: The Dilemma of the American High School.* Boston: Houghton Mifflin, 1984.

Stewart, D. "Administrative Models: The Disciplines." In T. L. Gross (ed.), *Our Mutual Estate: Schools/College/Business Partnerships.* Purchase, N.Y.: SUNY Purchase, 1987.

Trubowitz, S. *When a College Works with a Public School: A Case Study of School-College Collaboration.* Boston: Institute for Responsive Education, 1984.

Tyack, D. *The One Best System: A History of American Urban Education.* Cambridge, Mass.: Harvard University Press, 1979.

Usdan, M. *School Boards.* Washington, D.C.: Institute for Educational Leadership, 1987.

Wilbur, F. "High School-College Partnerships Can Work!" *Educational Record,* 62 (2), Spring 1981, pp. 38–44.

Wilbur, F. "Administrative Models: The Disciplines." In T. L. Gross (ed.), *Our Mutual Estate: Schools/College/Business Partnerships.* Purchase, N.Y.: SUNY Purchase, 1987.

Wilbur, F., Lambert, M., Young, M. J. *The National Directory of School-College Partnership: Current Models and Practices.* Washington, D.C.: American Association of Higher Education, 1987.

Williams, R. "Why Children Should Draw: The Surprising Link Between Art and Learning." *Saturday Review,* Sept. 3, 1977, pp. 10–16.

Wlodkowski, R. J. *Enhancing Adult Motivation to Learn: A Guide to Improving Instruction and Increasing Learner Achievement.* San Francisco: Jossey-Bass, 1985.

Wolf, D. *Academic Preparation in the Arts.* New York: College Board, 1985.

Woodside, W. *SUNY Purchase Westchester School Partnership Program Announcement.* March 16, 1984.

Woodside, W. *Corporate Leadership for Public Education.* An Occasional Paper on Leadership Issues. Washington, D.C.: Institute for Educational Leadership, 1986.

Index

RECEIVED
JUN 1990
Mission College
Learning Resource
Services